The Syrian Christ

Aspects of Middle Eastern Culture and Heritage in the Bible Gospels, Explained by a Lebanese Christian Theologian and Historian

Abraham Mitrie Rihbany

Published by Pantianos Classics

ISBN-13: 978-1-78987-249-1

First published in 1915

Contents

Preface

This little volume is sent forth in the confident hope that it may throw fresh light on the life and teachings of Christ, and facilitate for the general public the understanding of the Bible. As may be readily seen, from its perusal, the present work is not intended to be a commentary on the Bible, nor even an exhaustive study of the subject with which it deals. That it leaves many things to be desired is very evident to the author, who fears that his book will be remembered by its readers more by the things it lacks than by the things it contains.

Yet, from the cordial reception with which the opening chapters of this publication (which made their first appearance in the *Atlantic Monthly*) met from readers, of various religious affiliations, the author has been encouraged to believe that his aim has not only been clearly discerned, but thoroughly approved. The books which undertake the systematic "expounding of the Scriptures" are a host which no man can number, nor is there any lack of "spiritual lessons drawn from the Bible." Therefore, as one of the Master's fellow countrymen, and one who has enjoyed about twenty years of service in the American pulpit, I have for several years entertained the growing conviction that such a book as this was really needed. Not, however, as one more commentary, but as an Oriental guide to afford Occidental readers of the Bible a more intimate view of the original intellectual and social environment of this sacred literature. So what I have to offer here is a series of suggestions, and not of technically wrought Bible lessons.

The need of the Western readers of the Bible is, in my judgment, to enter sympathetically and intelligently into the atmosphere in which the books of the Scriptures first took form: to have real intellectual, as well as spiritual, fellowship with those Orientals who sought earnestly in their own way to give tangible form to those great spiritual truths which have been, and ever shall be, humanity's most precious heritage.

My task has not been a light one. It is comparatively easy to take isolated Bible texts and explain them, treating each passage as a detached unit. But when one undertakes to group a large number of passages which never were intended to be gathered together and treated as the kindred thoughts of an essay, the task becomes rather difficult. How far I have succeeded in my effort to relate the passages I have treated in this book to one another according to their intellectual and social affinities, the reader is in a better position to judge than I am.

It may not be absolutely necessary for me to say that infallibility cannot justly be ascribed to any author, nor claimed by him, even when writing of his own experiences, and the social environment in which he was born and brought up.

However, in Yankee, not in Oriental, fashion, I will say that *to the best of my knowledge* the statements contained in this book are correct.

Finally, I deem it necessary before I bring this preface to a close to sound a note of warning. So I will say that the Orientals' extensive use of figurative speech should by no means be allowed to carry the idea that *all* Oriental speech is figurative. This manner of speech, which is common to all races of men, is only *more extensively* used by Orientals than by Occidentals. I could wish, however, that the learned theologians had suspected more strongly the literal accuracy of Oriental utterances, and had thus been saved at times from founding a huge doctrinal structure on a figure of speech.

Notwithstanding all this, the Gospel and the Christian faith still live and bless and cheer the hearts and minds of men. As an Oriental by birth, and as an American from choice, I feel profoundly grateful that I have been enabled to render this modest service to the Churches of America, and to present this book as an offering of love and homage to my Master, the Syrian Christ.

ABRAHAM MITRIE RIHBANY
BOSTON, MASSACHUSETTS.

Part One - The Syrian Christ

Chapter One - Son of the East

Jesus Christ, the incarnation of the spirit of God, seer, teacher of the verities of the spiritual life, and preacher of the fatherhood of God and the brotherhood of man, is, in a higher sense, "a man without a country." As a prophet and a seer Jesus belongs to all races and all ages. Wherever the minds of men respond to simple truth, wherever the hearts of men thrill with pure love, wherever a temple of religion is dedicated to the worship of God and the service of man, there is Jesus' country and there are his friends. Therefore, in speaking of Jesus as the son of a certain country, I do not mean in the least to localize his Gospel, or to set bounds and limits to the flow of his spirit and the workings of his love.

Nor is it my aim in these chapters to imitate the astute theologians by wrestling with the problem of Jesus' personality. To me the secret of personality, human and divine, is an impenetrable mystery. My more modest purpose in this writing is to remind the reader that, whatever else Jesus was, as regards his modes of thought and life and his method of teaching, he was a Syrian of the Syrians. According to authentic history Jesus never saw any other country than Palestine. There he was born; there he grew up to manhood, taught his Gospel, and died for it.

It is most natural, then, that Gospel truths should have come down to the succeeding generations—and to the nations of the West—cast in Oriental moulds of thought, and intimately intermingled with the simple domestic and social habits of Syria. The gold of the Gospel carries with it the sand and dust of its original home.

From the foregoing, therefore, it may be seen that my reason for undertaking to throw fresh light on the life and teachings of Christ, and other portions of the Bible whose correct understanding depends on accurate knowledge of their original environment, is not any claim on my part to great learning or a profound insight into the spiritual mysteries of the Gospel. The real reason is rather an accident of birth. From the fact that I was born not far from where the Master was born, and brought up under almost the identical conditions under which he lived, I have an "inside view" of the Bible which, by the nature of things, a Westerner cannot have. And I know that the conditions of life in Syria of to-day are essentially as they were in the time of Christ, not from the study of the mutilated tablets of the archæologist and the antiquarian, precious as such discoveries are, but from the simple fact that, as a sojourner in this Western world, whenever I open my Bible it reads like a letter from home.

Its unrestrained effusiveness of expression; its vivid, almost flashy and fantastic imagery; its naïve narrations; the rugged unstudied simplicity of its parables; its unconventional (and to the more modest West rather unseemly) portrayal of certain human relations; as well as its all-permeating spiritual mysticism,—so far as these qualities are concerned, the Bible might all have been written in my primitive village home, on the western slopes of Mount Lebanon some thirty years ago.

Nor do I mean to assert or even to imply that the Western world has never succeeded in knowing the mind of Christ. Such an assertion would do violent injustice, not only to the Occidental mind, but to the Gospel itself as well, by making it an enigma, utterly foreign to the native spirituality of the majority of mankind. But what I have learned from intimate associations with the Western mind, during almost a score of years in the American pulpit, is that, with the exception of the few specialists, it is extremely difficult, if not impossible, for a people to understand fully a literature which has not sprung from that people's own racial life. As a repository of divine revelation the Bible knows no geographical limits. Its spiritual truths are from God to man. But as a literature the Bible is an imported article in the Western world, especially in the home of the Anglo-Saxon race. The language of the Scriptures, the mentality and the habits of life which form the setting of their spiritual precepts, and the mystic atmosphere of those precepts themselves, have come forth from the soul of a people far removed from the races of the West in almost all the modes of its earthly life.

You cannot study the life of a people successfully from the outside. You may by so doing succeed in discerning the few fundamental traits of character in their local colors, and in satisfying your curiosity with surface observations of the general modes of behavior; but the little things, the common things, those subtle connectives in the social vocabulary of a people, those agencies which are born and not made, and which give a race its rich distinctiveness, are bound to elude your grasp. There is so much in the life of a people which a stranger to that people must receive by way of unconscious absorption. Like a little child, he must learn so many things by involuntary imitation. An outside observer, though wise, is only a photographer. He deals with externals. He can be converted into an artist and portray the life of a race by working from the soul outward, only through long, actual, and sympathetic associations with that race.

From the foregoing it may be seen that I deem it rather hazardous for a six-weeks tourist in that country to publish a book on the *life* of Syria. A first-class camera and "an eye to business" are hardly sufficient qualifications for the undertaking of such a task. It is very easy, indeed, to take a photograph, but not so easy to relate such a picture to the inner life of a race, and to know what moral and social forces lie behind such externals. The hasty traveler may easily state what certain modes of thought and life in a strange land mean to *him*, but does that necessarily mean that *his* understanding of such things is also the understanding of the *people* of that land themselves?

8

With the passing of the years, this thought gains in significance with me, as a Syrian immigrant. At about the end of my second year of residence in this country, I felt confident that I could write a book on America and the Americans whose accuracy no one could challenge. It was so easy for me to grasp the significance of certain general aspects of American life that I felt I was fully competent to state how the American people lived, what their racial, political, and religious tendencies were, what their idioms of speech meant, and to interpret their amorous, martial, dolorous, and joyous moods with perfect accuracy and ease. But now, after a residence of about twenty-four years in America—years which I have spent in most intimate association with Americans, largely of the "original stock"—I do not feel half so confident that I am qualified to write such a book. The more intimate I become with American thought, the deeper I penetrate the American spirit, the more enlightened my associations become with American fathers, mothers, and children in the joys and sorrows of life, the more fully do I realize how extremely difficult, if not impossible, it is for one to interpret successfully the life of an alien people before one has actually *lived it* himself.

Many Westerners have written very meritorious books on the thought and life of the East. But these are not of the "tourist" type. Such writers have been those who, first, had the initial wisdom to realize that the beggars for *bakhsheesh* in the thoroughfares of Syrian cities, and those who hitch a woman with an ox to the plough in some dark recesses of Palestine, did not possibly represent the deep soul of that ancient East, which gave birth to the Bible and to the glorious company of prophets, apostles, and saints. Second, such writers knew, also, that the fine roots of a people's life do not lie on the surface. Such feeders of life are both deep and fine; not only long residence among a people, but intimate association and genuine sympathy with them are necessary to reveal to a stranger the hidden meaning of their life. Social life, like biological life, energizes from within, and from within it must be studied.

And it is those common things of Syrian life, so indissolubly interwoven with the spiritual truths of the Bible, which cause the Western readers of holy writ to stumble, and which rob those truths for them of much of their richness. By sheer force of genius, the aggressive, systematic Anglo-Saxon mind seeks to press into logical unity and creedal uniformity those undesigned, artless, and most natural manifestations of Oriental life, in order to "understand the Scriptures."

"Yet show I unto you a more excellent way," by personally conducting you into the inner chambers of Syrian life, and showing you, if I can, how simple it is for a humble fellow countryman of Christ to understand those social phases of the Scriptural passages which so greatly puzzle the august minds of the West.

Chapter Two - Birth of A Man Child

In the Gospel story of Jesus' life there is not a single incident that is not in perfect harmony with the prevailing modes of thought and the current speech of the land of its origin. I do not know how many times I heard it stated in my native land and at our own fireside that heavenly messengers in the forms of patron saints or angels came to pious, childless wives, in dreams and visions, and cheered them with the promise of maternity. It was nothing uncommon for such women to spend a whole night in a shrine "wrestling in prayer," either with the blessed Virgin or some other saint, for such a divine assurance; and I remember a few of my own kindred to have done so.

Perhaps the most romantic religious practice in this connection is the *zeara*. Interpreted literally, the word *zeara* means simply a visit. In its social use it is the equivalent of a call of long or short duration. But religiously the *zeara* means a pilgrimage to a shrine. However, strictly speaking, the word "pilgrimage" means to the Syrians a journey of great religious significance whose supreme purpose is the securing of a blessing for the pilgrim, with no reference to a special need. The *zeara* is a pilgrimage with a specific purpose. The *zayir* (visitor to a shrine) comes seeking either to be healed of a certain ailment, to atone for a sin, or to be divinely helped in some other way. Unlike a pilgrimage also, a *zeara* may be made by one person in behalf of another. When, for example, a person is too ill to travel, or is indifferent to a spiritual need which such a visit is supposed to fill, his parents or other close friends may make a *zeara* in his behalf. But much more often a *zeara* is undertaken by women for the purpose of securing the blessing of fecundity, or consecrating an approaching issue of wedlock (if it should prove to be a male) to God, and to the patron saint of the visited sanctuary.

Again the word "pilgrimage" is used only to describe a visit by a Christian to Jerusalem, or by a Mohammedan to Mecca, while the *zeara* describes a visit to any one of the lesser shrines.

The happy journey is often made on foot, the parties most concerned walking all the way "on the flesh of their feet"; that is, with neither shoes nor sandals on. This great sacrifice is made as a mark of sincere humility which is deemed to be pleasing to God and his holy saints. However, the wearing of shoes and even the use of mounts is not considered a sinful practice on such occasions, and is indulged in by many of the well-to-do families. The state of the heart is, of course, the chief thing to be considered.

In the fourth chapter of the Second Book of Kings we are told that "the Shunammite woman" used an ass when she sought Elisha to restore her dead son to her. In the twenty-second verse (the Revised Version), we are told, "And she called unto her husband, and said, Send me, I pray thee, one of the servants, and one of the asses, that I may run to the man of God, and come again.... Then she saddled an ass, and said to her servant, Drive, and go forward; slacken me not the riding, except I bid thee. So she went, and came unto the man of God to mount Carmel."

Fasting and prayer on the way are often pronounced phases of a *zeara*. However, wine-drinking by the men in the company and noisy gayety are not deemed altogether incompatible with the solemnity of the occasion. The pious visitors carry with them presents to the abbot and to the monks who serve the shrine. A silver or even gold candlestick, or a crown of either metal for the saint, is also carried to the altar. The young mother in whose behalf the *zeara* is undertaken is tenderly cared for by every member of the party. She is "the chosen vessel of the Lord."

The *zûwar* (visitors) remain at the holy shrine for one or two nights, or until the "presence" is revealed; that is, until the saint manifests himself. The prayerfully longed-for manifestation comes almost invariably in a dream, either to the mother or some other worthy in the party. How like the story of Joseph all this is! In the first chapter of St. Matthew's Gospel, the twentieth verse, it is said of Joseph, "But while he thought on these things, behold, the angel of the Lord appeared unto him in a dream, saying, Joseph, thou son of David, fear not to take unto thee Mary thy wife: for that which is conceived in her is of the Holy Ghost. And she shall bring forth a son, and thou shalt call his name Jesus; for he shall save his people from their sins."

In this manner the promise is made to the waiting mother, who "keeps these things, and ponders them in her heart."

The promise thus secured, the mother and the father vow that the child shall be a *nedher*; that is, consecrated to the saint who made the promise to the mother. The vow may mean one of several things. Either that a sum of money be "given to the saint" upon the advent of the child, or that the child be carried to the same sanctuary on another *zeara* with gifts, and so forth, or that his hair will not be cut until he is seven years old, and then cut for the first time before the image of his patron saint at the shrine, or some other act of pious fulfillment.

The last form of a vow, the consecration of the hair of the head for a certain period, is practiced by men of all ages. The vow is made as a petition for healing from a serious illness, rescue from danger, or purely as an act of consecration. In the eighteenth chapter of the Book of Acts, the eighteenth verse, we have the statement: "And Paul after this tarried there yet a good while, and then took his leave of the brethren, and sailed thence into Syria, and with him Priscilla and Aquila; *having shorn his head in Cenchrea: for he had a vow.*" It was also in connection with this practice that Paul was induced by the "brethren" at Jerusalem to make a compromise which cost him dearly. In the twenty-first chapter of Acts, the twenty-third verse, we are told that those brethren said to Paul, "We have four men who have a vow on them; them take, and purify thyself with them, and be at charges for them, that they may *shave their heads.*"

The last service of this kind which I attended in Syria was for a cousin of mine, a boy of twelve, who was a *nedher*, or as the word is rendered in the English Bible, a Nazarite. We assembled in the church of St. George of Sûk.

11

The occasion was very solemn. A mass was celebrated after the order of the Greek Orthodox Church. Near the close of the service the tender lad was brought by his parents in front of the Royal Door at the altar. While repeating a prayer, the priest cut the hair on the crown of the boy's head with the scissors, in the shape of a cross. The simple act released the child and his parents of their solemn vow.

"Twentieth-century culture" is prone to call all such practices superstitions. So they are to a large extent. But I deem it the higher duty of this culture to *interpret* sympathetically rather than to condemn superstition in a sweeping fashion. I am a lover of a rational theology and a reasonable faith, but I feel that in our enthusiasm for such a theology and such a faith we often fail to appreciate the deep spiritual longing which is expressed in superstitious forms of worship. What is there in such religious practices as those I have mentioned but the expression of the heart-burning of those parents for the spiritual welfare and security of their children? What do we find here but evidences of a deep and sincere yearning for divine blessings to come upon the family and the home? Thoughts of God at the marriage altar; thoughts of God when the promise of parenthood becomes evident; thoughts of God when a child comes into the world; thoughts of God and of his holy prophets and saints as friends and companions in all the changes and chances of the world. Here the challenge to modern rationalism is not to content itself with rebuking superstitions, but to give the world deeper spiritual visions than those which superstitions reveal, and to compass childhood and youth by the gracious presence of the living God.

In a most literal sense we always understood the saying of the psalmist, "Children are a heritage from the Lord." Above and beyond all natural agencies, it was He who turned barrenness to fecundity and worked the miracle of birth. To us every birth was miraculous, and childlessness an evidence of divine disfavor. From this it may be inferred how tenderly and reverently agreeable to the Syrian ear is the angel's salutation to Mary, "Hail, thou that art highly favored, the Lord is with thee; blessed art thou among women!—Behold thou shalt conceive in thy womb and bring forth a son." [1]

A miracle? Yes. But a miracle means one thing to your Western science, which seeks to know what nature is and does by dealing with secondary causes, and quite another thing to an Oriental, to whom God's will is the law and gospel of nature. In times of intellectual trouble this man takes refuge in his all-embracing faith,—the faith that to God all things are possible.

The Oriental does not try to meet an assault upon his belief in miracles by seeking to establish the historicity of concrete reports of miracles. His poetical, mystical temperament seeks its ends in another way. Relying upon his fundamental faith in the omnipotence of God, he throws the burden of proof upon his assailant by challenging him to substantiate his *denial* of the miracles. So did Paul (in the twenty-sixth chapter of the Book of Acts) put his opponents at a great disadvantage by asking, "Why should it be thought a thing incredible with you, that God should raise the dead?"

But the story of Jesus' birth and kindred Bible records disclose not only the predisposition of the Syrian mind to accept miracles as divine acts, without critical examination, but also its attitude toward conception and birth,—an attitude which differs fundamentally from that of the Anglo-Saxon mind. With the feeling of one who has been reminded of having ignorantly committed an improper act, I remember the time when kind American friends admonished me not to read from the pulpit such scriptural passages as detailed the accounts of conception and birth, but only to allude to them in a general way. I learned in a very short time to obey the kindly advice, but it was a long time before I could swing my psychology around and understand why in America such narratives were so greatly modified in transmission.

The very fact that such stories are found in the Bible shows that in my native land no such sifting of these narratives is ever undertaken when they are read to the people. From childhood I had been accustomed to hear them read at our church, related at the fireside, and discussed reverently by men and women at all times and places. There is nothing in the phraseology of such statements which is not in perfect harmony with the common, everyday speech of my people.

To the Syrians, as I say, "children are a heritage from the Lord." From the days of Israel to the present time, barrenness has been looked upon as a sign of divine disfavor, an intolerable calamity. Rachel's cry, "Give me children, or else I die," [2] does not exaggerate the agony of a childless Syrian wife. When Rebecca was about to depart from her father's house to become Isaac's wife, her mother's ardent and effusively expressed wish for her was, "Be thou the mother of thousands of millions." [3] This mother's last message to her daughter was not spoken in a corner. I can see her following the bride to the door, lifting her open palms and turning her face toward heaven, and making her affectionate petition in the hearing of a multitude of guests, who must have echoed her words in chorus.

In the congratulations of guests at a marriage feast the central wish for the bridegroom and bride is invariably thus expressed: "May you be happy, live long, and have many children!" And what contrasts very sharply with the American reticence in such matters is the fact that shortly after the wedding, the friends of the young couple, both men and women, begin to ask them about their "prospects" for an heir. No more does a prospective mother undertake in any way to disguise the signs of the approaching event, than an American lady to conceal her engagement ring. Much mirth is enjoyed in such cases, also, when friends and neighbors, by consulting the stars, or computing the number of letters in the names of the parents and the month in which the miracle of conception is supposed to have occurred, undertake to foretell whether the promised offspring will be a son or a daughter. In that part of the country where I was brought up, such wise prognosticators believed, and made us all believe, that if the calculations resulted in an odd number the birth would be a son, but if in an even number, a daughter, which, as a rule, is not considered so desirable.

13

Back of all these social traits, and beyond the free realism of the Syrian in speaking of conception and birth, lies a deeper fact. To Eastern peoples, especially the Semites, reproduction in all the world of life is profoundly sacred. It is God's life reproducing itself in the life of man and in the living world below man; therefore the evidences of this reproduction should be looked upon and spoken of with rejoicing.

Notwithstanding the many and fundamental intellectual changes which I have undergone in this country of my adoption, I count as among the most precious memories of my childhood my going with my father to the vineyard, just as the vines began to "come out," and hearing him say as he touched the swelling buds, "Blessed be the Creator. He is the Supreme Giver. May He protect the blessed increase." Of this I almost always think when I read the words of the psalmist, "The earth is the Lord's and the fullness thereof!"

Now I do not feel at all inclined to say whether the undisguised realism of the Orientals in speaking of reproduction is better than the delicate reserve of the Anglo-Saxons. In fact, I have been so reconstructed under Anglo-Saxon auspices as to feel that the excessive reserve of this race with regard to such things is not a serious fault, but rather the defect of a great virtue. My purpose is to show that the unreconstructed Oriental, to whom reproduction is the most sublime manifestation of God's life, cannot see why one should be ashamed to speak anywhere in the world of the fruits of wedlock, of a "woman with child." One might as well be ashamed to speak of the creative power as it reveals itself in the gardens of roses and the fruiting trees.

Here we have the background of the stories of Sarah, when the angel-guest prophesied fecundity for her in her old age; of Rebecca, and the wish of her mother for her, that she might become "the mother of thousands"; of Elizabeth, when the "babe leaped in her womb," as she saw her cousin Mary; and of the declaration of the angel to Joseph's spouse; "Thou shalt conceive in thy womb and bring forth a son."

Here it is explained, also, why upon the birth of a "man-child," well-wishers troop into the house,—even on the very day of birth,—bring their presents, and congratulate the parents on the divine gift to them. It was because of this custom that those strangers, the three "Wise Men" and Magi of the Far East, were permitted to come in and see the little Galilean family, while the mother was yet in childbed. So runs the Gospel narrative: "And when they were come into the house, they saw the young child with Mary his mother, and fell down and worshipped him: and when they had opened their treasures, they presented unto him gifts,—gold, frankincense, and myrrh." [4]

So also were the humble shepherds privileged to see the wondrous child shortly after birth. "And it came to pass, as the angels were gone away from them into heaven, the shepherds said one to another, Let us now go to Bethlehem, and see this thing which is come to pass, which the Lord hath made known unto us. And they came with haste, and found Mary and Joseph and the babe lying in a manger." [5]

In the twelfth verse of the second chapter of the Gospel of St. Luke, the English version says, "And this shall be a sign unto you; ye shall find a babe wrapped in swaddling clothes, lying in a manger." Here the word "clothes" is somewhat misleading. The Arabic version gives a perfect rendering of the fact by saying, "Ye shall find a *swaddled* babe, *laid* in a manger."

According to general Syrian custom, in earliest infancy a child is not really clothed, it is only swaddled. Upon birth the infant is washed in tepid water by the midwife, then salted, or rubbed gently with salt pulverized in a stone mortar especially for the occasion. (The salt commonly used in Syrian homes is coarse-chipped.) Next the babe is sprinkled with *rehan*,—a powder made of dried myrtle leaves,—and then swaddled.

The swaddle is a piece of stout cloth about a yard square, to one corner of which is attached a long narrow band. The infant, with its arms pressed close to its sides, and its feet stretched full length and laid close together, is wrapped in the swaddle, and the narrow band wound around the little body, from the shoulders to the ankles, giving the little one the exact appearance of an Egyptian mummy. Only a few of the good things of this mortal life were more pleasant to me when I was a boy than to carry in my arms a swaddled babe. The "salted" and "peppered" little creature felt so soft and so light, and was so appealingly helpless, that to cuddle it was to me an unspeakable benediction.

Such was the "babe of Bethlehem" that was sought by the Wise Men and the shepherds in the wondrous story of the Nativity.

And in describing such Oriental customs it may be significant to point out that, in certain localities in Syria, to say to a person that he was not "salted" upon birth is to invite trouble. Only a *bendûq*, or the child of an unrecognized father, is so neglected. And here may be realized the full meaning of that terrible arraignment of Jerusalem in the sixteenth chapter of the Book of Ezekiel. The Holy City had done iniquity, and therefore ceased to be the legitimate daughter of Jehovah. So the prophet cries, "The Lord came unto me, saying, Son of man, cause Jerusalem to know her abominations, and say, Thus saith the Lord God unto Jerusalem; Thy birth and thy nativity are of the land of Canaan; thy father was an Amorite, and thy mother a Hittite. And as for thy nativity, in the day thou wast born—neither wast thou washed in water to supple [6] thee; *thou wast not salted at all, nor swaddled at all.* No eye pitied thee, to do any of these things for thee, to have compassion upon thee; but thou wast cast out in the open field, to the loathing of thy person, in the day thou wast born."

[1] Luke i: 28, 31.
[2] Gen. xxx; 1.
[3] Gen. xxiv: 60.

[4] Matt. ii: 11.
[5] Luke ii: 15-16.
[6] "Cleanse" in the Revised Version.

Chapter Three - The Star

How natural to the thought of the East the story of the "star of Bethlehem" is! To the Orientals "the heavens declare the glory of God," and the stars reveal many wondrous things to men. They are the messengers of good and evil, and objects of the loftiest idealization, as well as of the crudest superstitions. Those who have gazed upon the stars in the deep, clear Syrian heavens can find no difficulty in entering into the spirit of the majestic strains of the writer of the eighth Psalm. "When I consider thy heavens," says this ancient singer, "the work of thy fingers, the moon and the stars, which thou hast ordained; what is man, that thou art mindful of him? and the son of man, that thou visitest him?" Deeps beyond deeps are revealed through that dry, soft, and clear atmosphere of the "land of promise," yet the constellations seem as near to the beholder as parlor lamps. "My soul longeth" for the vision of the heavens from the heights of my native Lebanon, and the hills of Palestine. It is no wonder to me that my people have always considered the stars as guides and companions, and as awe-inspiring manifestations of the Creator's power, wisdom, and glory. "The heavens declare the glory of God; and the firmament sheweth his handywork. Day unto day uttereth speech and night unto night sheweth knowledge." [1]

So great is the host of the stars seen by the naked eye in that land that the people of Syria have always likened a great multitude to the stars of heaven or the sand of the sea. Of a great assemblage of people we always said, "They are *methel-ennijoom*—like the stars" (in number). So it is written in the twenty-eighth chapter of Deuteronomy, the sixty-second verse, "And ye shall be left few in number, whereas ye were *as the stars of heaven for multitude*; because thou wouldst not obey the voice of the Lord thy God." According to that great narrative in Genesis, God promised Abraham that his progeny would be as the stars in number. In the fifteenth chapter, the fifth verse, it is said, "And he brought him forth abroad, and said, Look now toward heaven, and tell the stars, if thou be able to number them: and he said unto him, So shall thy seed be." In speaking of the omniscience of God the writer of the one hundred and forty-seventh Psalm says, "He telleth the number of the stars; he calleth them all by their names. Great is our Lord, and of great power: his understanding is infinite."

But the numberless lights of the firmament were brought even closer to us through the belief that they had vital connection with the lives of men on the earth. I was brought up to believe that every human being had a star in heaven which held the secret of his destiny and which watched over him wherever he went. In speaking of an amiable person it is said, "His star is attractive" (*nejmo jeddeeb*). Persons love one another when "their stars are in harmony." A person is in unfavorable circumstances when his star is in the sphere of "misfortune" (*nehiss*), and so forth. The stars indicated the time to us when we were traveling by night, marked the seasons, and thus fulfilled their Creator's purpose by serving "for signs, and for seasons, and for days and years."

In every community we had "star-gazers" who could tell each person's star. We placed much confidence in such mysterious men, who could "arrest" an absent person's star in its course and learn from it whether it was well or ill with the absent one.

Like a remote dream, it comes to me that as a child of about ten I went out one night with my mother to seek a "star-gazer" to locate my father's star and question the shining orb about him. My father had been away from home for some time, and owing to the meagerness of the means of communication in that country, especially in those days, we had no news of him at all. During that afternoon my mother said that she felt "heavy-hearted" for no reason that she knew; therefore she feared that some ill must have befallen the head of our household, and sought to "know" whether her fear was well grounded. The "star-arrester," leaning against an aged mulberry tree, turned his eyes toward the stellar world, while his lips moved rapidly and silently as if he were repeating words of awful import. Presently he said, "I see him. He is sitting on a cushion, leaning against the wall and smoking his *narghile*. There are others with him, and he is in his usual health." The man took pains to point out the "star" to my mother, who, after much sympathetic effort, felt constrained to say that she did see what the star-gazer claimed he saw. But at any rate, mother declared that she was no longer "heavy-hearted."

In my most keen eagerness to see my father and his *narghile* in the star, at least for mere intellectual delight, I clung to the arm of the reader of the heavens like a frightened kitten, and insisted upon "seeing." The harder he tried to shake me off, the deeper did my organs of apprehension sink into his sleeve. At last the combined efforts of my mother and the heir of the ancient astrologers forced me to believe that I was "too young to behold such sights."

It was the excessive leaning of his people upon such practices that led Isaiah to cry, "Thou art wearied in the multitude of thy counsels. Let now the astrologers, the star-gazers, the monthly prognosticators, stand up and save thee from these things that shall come upon thee. Behold, they shall be as stubble; the fire shall burn them; they shall not deliver themselves from the power of the flames."

Beyond all such crudities, however, lies the sublime and sustaining belief that the stars are alive with God. The lofty strains of such scriptural passages as the nineteenth Psalm and the beautiful story of the star of Bethlehem, indicate that to the Oriental mind the "hosts of heaven" are no mere masses of dust, but the agencies of the Creator's might and love. So the narrative of the Nativity in our Gospel sublimates the beliefs of the Orientals about God's purpose in those lights of the firmament, by making the guide of the Wise Men to the birthplace of the Prince of Peace a great star, whose pure and serene light symbolized the peace and holiness which, in the "fullness of time," his kingdom shall bring upon the earth.

17

The presentation of a child at the temple, or the "admittance of an infant into the Church," is one of the most tender, most beautiful, and most impressive services of my Mother Church—the Greek Orthodox. [2] It is held for every child born within that fold, in commemoration of the presentation of Jesus at the temple in Jerusalem. As Luke tells us (11:22), "And when the days of her purification according to the law of Moses were accomplished, they brought him to Jerusalem, to present him to the Lord."

The purification period "according to the law of Moses" is forty days. [3] Until this is "accomplished," the mother is not permitted to enter into the house of worship. As a general rule the baptismal service, which takes place any time between the eighth day and the fortieth day after birth, is held at the home. On the first Sabbath day after the "forty days," the mother carries the infant to the door of the church during mass, where the robed priest, who has been previously applied to for the sacred rite, meets the mother and receives the child in his arms. After making the sign of the cross with the child at the door, the priest says, "Now enters the servant of God [naming the child] into the Holy Church, in the name of the Father, and the Son, and the Holy Ghost. Amen." Then the priest walks into the church with the child, saying, in its behalf, "I will come into thy house in the multitude of thy mercy: and in thy fear will I worship toward thy holy temple." [4] As he approaches the center of the church, he says again, "Now enters the servant of God," etc. Then standing in the center of the church, and surrounded by the reverently silent congregation, the priest says again, in behalf of the child, "In the midst of the congregation will I praise thee, O Lord." [5] Again, in front of the Royal Gate (the central door in the *anastasis*, or partition which screens the altar from the congregation) the priest says for the third time, "Now enters the servant of God," etc. After this the priest carries the infant through the north door, which is to the left of the Royal Gate, into the *mizbeh*, which corresponds to the "holy place" in the ancient temple. Here he walks around the *maideh* (altar of sacrifice), makes the sign of the cross with the child, and walks out into the midst of the congregation, through the south door. In this position the priest utters as his final petition the words of the aged Simeon (Luke 11:29), "Lord, now lettest thou thy servant depart in peace, according to thy word: for mine eyes have seen thy salvation, which thou hast prepared before the face of all people; a light to lighten the gentiles, and the glory of thy people Israel." Then he delivers the child back to its mother. Female children are presented in front of the Royal Gate, but are not admitted into the *mizbeh*.

[1] Ps. xix: 1-2.
[2] See the author's autobiography, *A Far Journey*, p. 4.
[3] Lev. xii: 2-4.
[4] Ps. v: 7.
[5] Ps. xx: 22.

Chapter Four - Mystic Tones

I love to listen to the mystic tones of the Christmas carol. The story of the "star of Bethlehem" is the medium of transmission of those deeper strains which have come into the world through the soul of that ancient East. I love to mingle with the social joys of the Christmas season and its spirit of good-will, the mystic accents of the ancient seers who expressed in the rich narratives of the New Testament the deepest and dearest hopes of the soul.

I leave most respectfully to the "Biblical critic" the task of assigning to the narrative of the Nativity its rightful place in the history of the New Testament. My deep interest in this story centers in those spiritual ideals it reveals, which have through the ages exercised such beneficent influences over the minds of men. And I believe that both as a Christian and as an Oriental, I have a perfect right to be a mystic, after the wholesome New Testament fashion.

In the second chapter of St. Luke's Gospel the story of the Nativity is presented in a most exquisite poetical form. The vision of humble shepherds, wise men, and angels, mingling together in the joy of a new divine revelation, could have been caught only by a deep-visioned spiritual artist. Had this fragment of religious literature been discovered in this year of 1916, its appearance would have marked a significant epoch in the history of religion. It is the expression of a sublime and passionate desire of the soul for divine companionship and for infinite peace.

"And there were in the same country shepherds abiding in the field, keeping watch over their flocks by night.

"And, lo, the angel of the Lord came upon them, and the glory of the Lord shone round about them: and they were sore afraid.

"And the angel said unto them, Fear not; for, behold, I bring you good tidings of great joy, which shall be to all people.

"For unto you is born this day in the city of David a Savior, which is Christ the Lord.

"And this shall be a sign unto you; Ye shall find the babe wrapped in swaddling clothes, lying in a manger.

"And suddenly there was with the angel a multitude of the heavenly host praising God, and saying,

"Glory to God in the highest, and on earth peace, good will toward men."

When the angel delivered his message to the effect that God had visited his people in the person of the new-born Christ, then the humble, unlettered shepherds heard the heavenly song, which gave God the glory, and prophesied peace and good-will for all mankind. Could there be anything more profoundly and accurately interpretative of the deepest hopes of the human soul than this picture? Even the uncouth shepherds, being living souls, could realize that when the divine and the human met heaven and earth became one, and peace and good-will prevailed among men. What encouragement, what hope this vision holds out even to the humblest among men! What assurance that heaven with all its treasures of peace and love is so near to our dust!

"And the angel said unto them, Fear not: for, behold, I bring you glad tidings." The shepherds looked up to heaven through the eyes of all mankind. It was the upward look of a world-old hope. No soul ever looked up to heaven with different results. The divine response always is, "Fear not, for I bring you good tidings!" No soul ever needs to dwell in doubt and fear. No soul ever needs to be lonely and forlorn. Heaven has nothing for us but "good tidings of great joy." The higher powers are near at hand, and the soul of man may have invisible companions.

Again we learn from this New Testament passage that in the visit of the shepherds and the Wise Men to the holy child both were equally blest. Both those who were steeped in the wisdom of that ancient East and the simple-minded sons of the desert stood at the shrine of a holy personality as naked souls, divested of all artificial human distinctions. There were no "assigned" pews in that little shrine. All those who came into it by way of the heart received a blessing, and went away praising God. Here we have a foregleam of that longed-for kingdom of God—the home of all aspiring and seeking souls, regardless of rank and station.

"There is no great and no small
   To the soul that maketh all:
   And where it cometh, all things are;
   And it cometh everywhere."

The Christmas carol is dear to the human heart because it is a song of spiritual optimism. To pessimism the heavens are closed and silent; the world has no windows opening toward the Infinite. Pessimism cannot sing because it has no hope, and cannot pray because it has no faith.

And I deem it essential at this point to ask, Whither is the spirit of the present age leading us? Are we drifting away from the mount of vision? There seems to be but little room in this vast and complex life of ours for spiritual dreams and visions. The combination of our commercial activities and the never-ceasing whir of the wheels of our industries close up our senses to the intimate whisperings of the divine spirit. We see, but with the outward eye. We hear, but with the outward ear. Our inward senses are in grave danger of dying altogether from lack of exercise. The things of this life are too much with us, and they render us oblivious to the gracious beckonings of the higher world. Let not the lesser interests of this life close our hearing to the angel-song which never dies upon the air. The star of hope never sets, and God's revelations are from everlasting to everlasting.

Chapter Five - Filial Obedience

OF Jesus' life between the period spoken of in the narrative of the Nativity and the time when he appeared on the banks of the Jordan, seeking to be baptized by John, the New Testament says nothing. One single incident only is mentioned. When twelve years old, the boy Jesus went with his parents on a pilgrimage to Jerusalem. Annual pilgrimages to the great shrines are still very common in Syria. The Mohammedans go to Mecca, the Christians and the Jews to Jerusalem. But there are many other and more accessible sanctuaries which are frequented by the faithful in all those communions. However, a visit to any other sanctuary than Jerusalem and Mecca is called *zeara*, rather than a pilgrimage. The simple record of Jesus' pilgrimage to Jerusalem with his parents is that of a typical experience. In writing about it I seem to myself to be giving a personal reminiscence.

In the second chapter of the Gospel of Luke, the forty-first verse, it is said: "Now his parents went to Jerusalem every year at the feast of the passover. And when he was twelve years old, they went up to Jerusalem after the custom of the feast. And when they had fulfilled the days, as they returned, the child Jesus tarried behind in Jerusalem; and Joseph and his mother knew not of it. But they, supposing him to have been in the company, went a day's journey; and they sought him among their kinsfolk and acquaintance. And when they found him not, they turned back again to Jerusalem, seeking him."

In Syria male children are taken on a pilgrimage or *zeara*, and thus permitted to receive the blessing, which this pious act is supposed to bring upon them, as soon as they are able to make the journey. Full maturity is no essential condition. I went with my parents on two *zearas* before I was fifteen. At the present time there is no definite rule, at least among Christians, as to how many days should be spent at a sanctuary. Pilgrims usually "vow" to stay a certain number of days. In ancient Judaism, "the feast of the passover" occupied eight days, and it was that number of days which Mary and Joseph "fulfilled."

According to Luke, on their return journey to Nazareth Jesus' parents went a day's journey before they discovered that he was not with them. This phase of the story seems to have greatly puzzled the good old commentator, Adam Clarke. "Knowing what a treasure they possessed," he observes, "how could they be so long without looking on it? Where were the bowels and tender solicitude of the mother? Let them answer this question who can."

Clarke did not need to be so perplexed or so mystified. For one who knows the customs of the Syrians while on religious pilgrimages knows also that the experience of the "holy family" was not at all a strange one. The whole mystery is cleared up in the saying, "And they sought him among their kinsfolk and acquaintance." Kinsfolk and acquaintances travel in large groups, and the young pilgrims, such as the twelve-year-old Jesus, are considered safe so long as they keep in close touch with the company. On such journeys, parents may not see their sons for hours at a time. The homogeneous character of the group, and the sense of security which faith gives, especially at such times, present no occasion for anxiety concerning the dear ones.

The saying of Luke that Joseph and Mary "went a day's journey" before they discovered that Jesus was not in the company must, it seems to me, include also the time consumed in their return journey to Jerusalem to seek their son. Perhaps they discovered his absence about noontime when the company halted by a spring of water to partake of the *zad* (food for the way). At such a time families gather together to break bread. And what I feel certain of also is that the boy Jesus must have been with his parents when they first set out on their homeward journey early in the morning from Jerusalem, and that he detached himself from his kinsfolk and returned to the holy city shortly after the company had left that place. No Syrian family ever would start out on a journey before every one of its members had been accounted for. The evangelist's omission of these details is easily understood. His purpose was not to give a photographic account of all that happened on the way. It was rather to reveal the lofty spiritual ideals which led the boy Jesus to return to the temple, where he was found by his anxious parents "sitting in the midst of the doctors, both hearing them, and asking them questions."

In this brief but significant record of all the filial graces which Jesus must have possessed one only is mentioned in the second chapter of the Gospel of Luke, where it is stated that he went down to Nazareth with his parents "and was subject unto them."

This seemingly casual remark is full of significance. With us in Syria, *ta'at-el-walideen* (obedience to parents) has always been youth's crowning virtue. Individual initiative must not overstep the boundary line of this grace. Only in this way the patriarchal organization of the family can be kept intact. In my boyhood days in that romantic country, whenever my father took me with him on a "visit of homage" to one of the lords of the land, the most fitting thing such a dignitary could do to me was to place his hand upon my head and say with characteristic condescension, "Bright boy, and no doubt obedient to your parents."

As regards the grace of filial obedience, I am not aware of a definite break between the East and the West. But there is a vital difference. To an Oriental who has just come to this country, the American youth seem to be indifferent to filial obedience. The strong passion for freedom, the individualistic sense which is a pronounced characteristic of the aggressive Anglo-Saxon, and the economic stress which ever tends to scatter the family group, and which the East has never experienced so painfully as the West has, all convey the impression that parental love and filial obedience are fast disappearing from American society. But to those of us sons of the East who have intimate knowledge of the American family, its cohesion does not seem to be so alarmingly weak. The mad rush for "business success" is indeed a menace to the American home, but love and obedience are still vital forces in that home.

22

The terms "father," "mother," "brother," and "sister," have by no means lost their spiritual charms in American society. The deep affection in which the members of the better American family hold one another and the exquisite regard they have for one another command profound respect.

But the vital difference between the East and the West is that to Easterners filial obedience is more than a social grace and an evidence of natural affection. It is a *religious* duty of far-reaching significance. God commands it. "Thou shalt honor thy father and thy mother" is a divine command. The "displeasure" of a parent is as much to be feared as the wrath of God. This sense permeates Syrian society from the highest to the lowest of its ranks.

The explanation of the origin of sin in the third chapter of Genesis touches the very heart of this matter. The writer ascribes the "fall of man," not to any act which was in itself really harmful, but to disobedience. Adam was commanded by his divine parent not to eat of the "tree of knowledge of good and evil"; but he did eat, and consequently became a stranger to the blessings of his original home.

This idea of filial obedience has been at once the strength and weakness of Orientals. In the absence of the restraining interests of a larger social life this patriarchal rule has preserved the cohesion of the domestic and clannish group, and thus safeguarded for the people their primitive virtues. On the other hand, it has served to extinguish the spirit of progress, and has thus made Oriental life a monotonous repetition of antiquated modes of thought.

And it was indeed a great blessing to the world when Jesus broke away from mere formal obedience to parents, in the Oriental sense of the word, and declared, "Whosoever shall do the will of my Father in heaven, the same is my brother, and sister, and mother."

Chapter Six - Feast and Sacrament

Of Jesus' public ministry and his characteristics as an Oriental teacher, I shall speak in later chapters. Here I will give space only to a portrayal of the closing scenes in his personal career. The events of the "upper room" on Mount Zion, and of Gethsemane, are faithful photographs of striking characteristics of Syrian life.

The Last Supper was no isolated event in Syrian history. Its fraternal atmosphere, intimate associations, and sentimental intercourse are such as characterize every such gathering of Syrian friends, especially in the shadow of an approaching danger. From the simple "table manners" up to that touch of sadness and idealism which the Master gave that meal,—bestowing upon it the sacrificial character that has been its propelling force through the ages,—I find nothing which is not in perfect harmony with what takes place on such occasions in my native land. The sacredness of the Last Supper is one of the emphatic examples of how Jesus' life and words sanctified the commonest things of life. He was no inventor of new things, but a discoverer of the spiritual significance of things known to men to be ordinary.

The informal formalities of Oriental life are brimful of sentiment. The Oriental's chief concern in matters of conduct is not the correctness of the technique, but the cordiality of the deed. To the Anglo-Saxon the Oriental appears to be perhaps too cordial, decidedly sentimental, and over-responsive to the social stimulus. To the Oriental, on the other hand, the Anglo-Saxon seems in danger of becoming an unemotional intellectualist.

Be that as it may, the Oriental is never afraid to "let himself go" and to give free course to his feelings. The Bible in general and such portions of it as the story of the Last Supper in particular illustrate this phase of Oriental life.

In Syria, as a general rule, the men eat their fraternal feasts alone, as in the case of the Master and his disciples at the Last Supper, when, so far as the record goes, none of the women followers of Christ were present. They sit on the floor in something like a circle, and eat out of one or a few large, deep dishes. The food is lifted into the mouth, not with a fork or spoon,—except in the case of liquid food,—but with small "shreds" of thin bread. Even liquid food is sometimes "dipped up" with pieces of bread formed like the bowl of a spoon. Here may be readily understood Jesus' saying, "He that dippeth his hand with me in the dish, the same shall betray me." [1]

In his famous painting, The Last Supper, Leonardo da Vinci presents an Oriental event in an Occidental form. The high table, the chairs, the individual plates and drinking-glasses are European rather than Syrian appointments. From a historical standpoint, the picture is misleading. But Da Vinci's great production was not intended to be a historical, but a character, study. Such a task could not have been accomplished if the artist had presented the Master and his disciples as they really sat in the "upper room"—in a circle. He seats them on one side of the table, divides them into four groups of three each—two groups on each side of the Master. As we view the great painting, we feel the thrill of horror which agitated the loyal disciples when Jesus declared, "Verily, I say unto you, that one of you shall betray me." [2] The gestures, the sudden change of position, and the facial expression reveal the innermost soul of each disciple. This is the central purpose of the picture. The artist gave the event a European rather than an Oriental setting, in order to make it more intelligible to the people for whom it was intended.

But the appointments of the Great Supper were genuinely Oriental. The Master and his disciples sat on the floor and ate out of one or a few large, deep dishes. In Mark's account of that event [3] we read: "And when it was evening he cometh with the twelve. And as they sat and were eating, Jesus said, Verily I say unto you, One of you shall betray me, even he that *eateth* with me." The fact that they were *all* eating with him is shown in the statement, "They began to be sorrowful, and to say unto him, Is it I? And he said unto them, It is one of the twelve, he that dippeth with me in the dish."

The last sentence, "He that dippeth with me in the dish," has been con-strued to mean that it was Judas only (who was sitting near to Jesus) who was dipping in the dish out of which the Master was eating. This is altogether possible, but by no means certain. The fact is that according to Syrian cus-toms on such occasions each of the few large dishes contains a different kind of food. Each one of the guests is privileged to reach to any one of the dishes and dip his bread in it. From this it may be safely inferred that several or all of the disciples dipped *in turn* in the dish which was nearest to Jesus. The fact that the other disciples did not know whom their Master meant by his saying that one of them should betray him, even after he had said, "He that dippeth with me in the dish," shows plainly that Judas was eating in the same fashion as all the other disciples were.

Therefore the saying, "He that dippeth with me," etc., was that of disap-pointed love. It may be thus paraphrased: "I have loved you all alike. I have chosen you as my dearest friends. We have often broken bread and sorrowed and rejoiced together, yet one of you, my dear disciples, one who is now eat-ing with me *as the rest are*, intends to betray me!"

And that forlorn but glorious company who met in the upper room on Mount Zion on that historic night had certainly one cup out of which they drank. At our feasts we always drank the wine out of one and the same cup. We did not stay up nights thinking about microbes. To us the one cup meant fellowship and fraternal communion. The one who gives drink (*sacky*) fills the cup and passes it to the most honored member of the company first. He drinks the contents and returns the cup to the *sacky*, who fills it again and hands it to another member of the group, and so on, until all have been served once. Then the guests drink again by way of *nezel*. It is not easy to translate this word into English. The English word "treating" falls very short of expressing the affectionate regard which the *nezel* signifies. The one guest upon receiving the cup wishes for the whole company "health, happiness, and length of days." Then he singles out one of the group and begs him to accept the next cup that is poured as a pledge of his affectionate regard. The pourer complies with the request by handing the next cup to the person thus designated, who drinks it with the most effusive and affectionate reciproca-tion of his friend's sentiments. It is also customary for a gracious host to re-quest as a happy ending to the feast that the contents of one cup be drunk by the whole company as a seal of their friendship with one another. Each guest takes a sip and passes the cup to the one next to him until all have partaken of the "fruit of the vine."

I have no doubt that it was after this custom that the disciples drank when Jesus "took the cup, and when he had given thanks, he gave to them: and they *all* drank of it." [4]

No account of fraternal feasting in Syria can be complete without mention of the *zĭkreh* (remembrance). To be remembered by his friends after his de-parture from them is one of the Syrian's deepest and dearest desires. The *zĭkreh* plays a very important part in the literature of the East, and expresses the tenderest spirit of its poetry. The expressions "I remember," "remember me," "your remembrance," "the remembrance of those days" and like phrases are legion among the Syrians. "O friends," cries the Arabian poet, "let your remembrance of us be as constant as our remembrance of you; for such a remembrance brings near those that are far away."

Rarely do friends who have been feasting together part without this request being made by those of them who do not expect to meet with their friends again for a time. "Remember me when you meet again," is said by the departing friend with unspeakable tenderness. He is affectionately grateful also when he knows that he is held in remembrance by his friends. So St. Paul pours out his soul in grateful joy for his friends' remembrance of him. "But now when Timotheus came from you unto us, and brought us good tidings of your faith and charity, and that *ye have good remembrance of us always, desiring greatly to see us, as we also to see you.*" [5]

This affectionate request, "remember me," signifies, "I love you, therefore I am always with you." If we love one another, we cannot be separated from one another. The *z[]i]ikreh* is the bond of fraternity between us.

Was not this the very thing which the Master meant when he said, "This do in remembrance of me"? [6] The disciples were asked never to allow themselves to forget their Master's love for them and for the world: never to forget that if his love lived in their hearts he was always with them, present at their feasts, and in their struggles in the world to lead the world from darkness into light. "This do in remembrance of me," is therefore the equivalent of "Lo, I am with you alway, even unto the end of the world." [7]

"Now there was leaning on Jesus' bosom one of his disciples, whom Jesus loved." [8] The posture of the "beloved disciple," John,—so objectionable to Occidental taste,—is in perfect harmony with Syrian customs. How often have I seen men friends in such an attitude. There is not in it the slightest infringement of the rules of propriety; the act was as natural to us all as shaking hands. The practice is especially indulged in when intimate friends are about to part from one another, as on the eve of a journey, or when about to face a dangerous undertaking. They then sit with their heads leaning against each other, or the one's head resting upon the other's shoulder or breast.

They talk to one another in terms of unbounded intimacy and unrestrained affection. The expressions, "My brother," "My eyes," "My soul," "My heart," and the like, form the life-centers of the conversation. "My life, my blood are for you; take the very sight of my eyes, if you will!" And lookers-on say admiringly, "Behold, how they love one another! By the name of the Most High, they are closer than brothers."

Was it, therefore, strange that the Master, who knew the deepest secret of the divine life, and whose whole life was a living sacrifice, should say to his intimate friends, as he handed them the bread and the cup on that momentous night, "Take, eat; this is my body"; and "Drink ye all of it; for this is my blood"? Here again the Nazarene charged the ordinary words of friendly intercourse with rare spiritual richness and made the common speech of his people express eternal realities.

But let me here call attention to Da Vinci's master-stroke which changes for a moment John's posture and relieves the Last Supper of a feature which is so objectionable to Occidental taste. The artist seizes the moment when Peter pulled John from Jesus' breast by beckoning to the beloved disciple "that he should ask who it should be of whom he spoke" (the one who should betray him). John remains in the attitude of loving repose; he simply lifts his body for an instant, and inclines his head to hear Peter.

The treachery of Judas is no more an Oriental than it is a human weakness. Traitors can claim neither racial nor national refuge. They are fugitives in the earth. But in the Judas episode is involved one of the most tender, most touching acts of Jesus' whole life. To one familiar with the customs of the East, Jesus' handing the "sop" to his betrayer was an act of surpassing beauty and significance. In all my life in America I have not heard a preacher interpret this simple deed, probably because of lack of knowledge of its meaning in Syrian social intercourse.

"And when he had dipped the sop, he gave it to Judas Iscariot, the son of Simon." [9] At Syrian feasts, especially in the region where Jesus lived, such sops are handed to those who stand and serve the guests with wine and water. But in a more significant manner those morsels are exchanged by friends. Choice bits of food are handed to friends by one another, as signs of close intimacy. It is never expected that any person would hand such a sop to one for whom he cherishes no friendship.

I can never contemplate this act in the Master's story without thinking of "the love of Christ which passeth knowledge." To the one who carried in his mind and heart a murderous plot against the loving Master, Jesus handed the sop of friendship, the morsel which is never offered to an enemy. The rendering of the act in words is this: "Judas, my disciple, I have infinite pity for you. You have proved false, you have forsaken me in your heart; but I will not treat you as an enemy, for I have come, not to destroy, but to fulfill. Here is my sop of friendship, and 'that thou doest, do quickly.'"

Apparently Jesus' demeanor was so cordial and sympathetic that, as the evangelist tells us, "Now no man at the table knew for what intent he spake this unto him. For some of them thought, because Judas had the bag, that Jesus had said unto him, Buy those things that we have need of against the feast, or that he should give something to the poor." [10]

Thus in this simple act of the Master, so rarely noticed by preachers, we have perhaps the finest practical example of "Love your enemies" in the entire Gospel.

Is it therefore to be wondered at that in speaking of Judas, the writer of St. John's Gospel says, "And after the sop Satan entered into him"? For, how can one who is a traitor at heart reach for the gift of true friendship without being transformed into the very spirit of treason?

27

Again, Judas's treasonable kiss in Gethsemane was a perversion of an ancient, deeply cherished, and universally prevalent Syrian custom. In saluting one another, especially after having been separated for a time, men friends of the same social rank kiss one another on both cheeks, sometimes with very noisy profusion. When they are not of the same social rank, the inferior kisses the hand of the superior, while the latter at least pretends to kiss his dutiful friend upon the cheek. So David and Jonathan "kissed one another, until David exceeded." Paul's command, "Salute one another with a holy kiss," so scrupulously disobeyed by Occidental Christians, is characteristically Oriental. As a child I always felt a profound reverential admiration for that unreserved outpouring of primitive affections, when strong men "fell upon one another's neck" and kissed, while the women's eyes swam in tears of joy. The passionate, quick, and rhythmic exchange of affectionate words of salutation and kisses sounded, with perhaps a little less harmony, like an intermingling of vocal and instrumental music.

So Judas, when "forthwith he came to Jesus, and said, Hail, Master, and kissed him," [11] invented no new sign by which to point Jesus out to the Roman soldiers, but employed an old custom for the consummation of an evil design. Just as Jesus glorified the common customs of his people by using them as instruments of love, so Judas degraded those very customs by wielding them as weapons of hate.

[1] Matt. xxvi: 23.

[2] Matt. xxvi: 21.

[3] Revised Version, xiv: 17-20.

[4] Mark xiv: 23.

[5] 1 Thess. iii: 6.

[6] Luke xxii: 19.

[7] Matt. xxviii: 10.

[8] John xiii: 23.

[9] John xiii: 26.

[10] John xiii: 28, 29.

[11] Matt. xxvi: 49.

Chapter Seven - The Last Scene

Perhaps nowhere else in the New Testament do the fundamental traits of the Oriental nature find so clear an expression as in this closing scene of the Master's life. The Oriental's *dependence*, to which the world owes the loftiest and tenderest Scriptural passages, finds here its most glorious manifestations.

As I have already intimated, the Oriental is never afraid to "let himself go," whether in joy or sorrow, and to give vent to his emotions. It is of the nature of the Anglo-Saxon to suffer in silence, and to kill when he must, with hardly a word of complaint upon his lips or a ripple of excitement on his face. He disdains asking for sympathy. His severely individualistic tendencies and spirit of endurance convince him that he is "able to take care of himself." During my early years in this country the reserve of Americans in times of sorrow and danger, as well as in times of joy, was to me not only amazing, but appalling. Not being as yet aware of their inward fire and intensity of feeling, held in check by a strong bulwark of calm calculation, as an unreconstructed Syrian I felt prone to doubt whether they had any emotions to speak of.

It is not my purpose here to undertake a comparative critical study of these opposing traits, but to state that, for good or evil, the Oriental is preeminently a man who craves sympathy, yearns openly and noisily for companionship, and seeks help and support outside himself. Whatever disadvantages this trait may involve, it has been the one supreme qualification that has made the Oriental the religious teacher of the whole world. It was his childlike dependence on God that gave birth to the twenty-third and fifty-first Psalms, and made the Lord's Prayer the universal petition of Christendom. It was also this dependence on companionship, human and divine, which inspired the great commandments, "Thou shalt love the Lord thy God with all thy heart, and thy neighbor as thyself."

Now it is in the light of this fundamental Oriental trait that we must view Christ's utterances at the Last Supper and in Gethsemane. The record tells us that while at the Supper he said to his disciples, "With desire I have desired to eat this passover with you before I suffer," [1]—or, as the marginal note has it, "I have heartily desired," and so forth, which brings it nearer the original text. Again, "He was troubled in spirit, and testified and said, Verily, verily, I say unto you, that one of you shall betray me." "This is my body ... This is my blood ... Do this in remembrance of me." We must seek the proper setting for these utterances, not merely in the upper room in Zion, but in the deepest tendencies of the Oriental mind.

And the climax is reached in the dark hour of Gethsemane, in the hour of intense suffering, imploring need, and ultimate triumph in Jesus' surrender to the Father's will. How true to that demonstrative Oriental nature is the Scriptural record, "And being in an agony he prayed more earnestly: and his sweat was as it were great drops of blood falling down to the ground." [2]

The faithful and touching realism of the record here is an example of the childlike responsiveness of the Syrian nature to feelings of sorrow, no less striking than the experience itself. It seems to me that if an Anglo-Saxon teacher in similar circumstances had ever allowed himself to agonize and to sweat "as it were great drops of blood," his chronicler in describing the scene would have safeguarded the dignity of his race by simply saying that the distressed teacher was "visibly affected"!

The darkness deepened and the Master "took with him Peter and the two sons of Zebedee, and began to be sorrowful and very heavy. Then saith he unto them, My soul is exceeding sorrowful, even unto death; tarry ye here, and watch with me." [3] Three times did the Great Teacher utter that matchless prayer, whose spirit of fear as well as of trust vindicates the doctrine of the humanity of God and the divinity of man as exemplified in the person of Christ: "O my Father, if it be possible, let this cup pass from me: nevertheless not as I will, but as thou wilt!" [4]

The sharp contrast between the Semitic and the Anglo-Saxon temperament has led some unfriendly critics of Christ to state very complacently and confidently that he "simply broke down when the critical hour came." In this assertion I find a very pronounced misapprehension of the facts. If my knowledge of the traits of my own race is to be relied on, then in trying to meet this assertion I feel that I am entitled to the consideration of one who speaks with something resembling authority.

The simple fact is that while in Gethsemane, as indeed everywhere else throughout his ministry, Jesus was not in the position of one trying to "play the hero." His companions were his intimate earthly friends and his gracious heavenly Father, and to them he spoke as an Oriental would speak to those dear to him,—*just as he felt*, with not a shadow of show or sham. His words were not those of weakness and despair, but of confidence and affection. The love of his friends and the love of his Father in heaven were his to draw upon in his hour of trial, with not the slightest artificial reserve. How much better and happier this world would be if we all dealt with one another and with God in the warm, simple, and pure love of Christ!

As the life and words of Christ amply testify, the vision of the Oriental has been to teach mankind not science, logic, or jurisprudence, but a simple, loving, childlike faith in God. Therefore, before we can fully know our Master as the cosmopolitan Christ, we must first know him as the Syrian Christ.

[1] Luke xxii: 15.
[2] Luke xxii: 44.

[3] Matt. xxvi: 37-38.
[4] *Ibid.* 39.

Part Two - The Oriental Manner of Speech

Chapter One - Daily Language

The Oriental I have in mind is the Semite, the dweller of the Near East, who, chiefly through the Bible, has exerted an immense influence on the life and literature of the West. The son of the Near East is more emotional, more intense, and more communicative than his Far-Eastern neighbors. Although very old in point of time, his temperament remains somewhat juvenile, and his manner of speech intimate and unreserved.

From the remote past, even to this day, the Oriental's manner of speech has been that of a worshipper, and not that of a business man or an industrial worker in the modern Western sense. To the Syrian of to-day, as to his ancient ancestors, life, with all its activities and cares, revolves around a religious center.

Of course this does not mean that his religion has not always been beset with clannish limitations and clouded by superstitions, or that the Oriental has always had a clear, active consciousness of the sanctity of human life. But it does mean that this man, serene or wrathful, at work or at play, praying or swearing, has never failed to believe that he is overshadowed by the All-seeing God. He has never ceased to cry: "O Lord, Thou hast searched me, and known me. Thou knowest my downsitting and mine uprising; Thou understandest my thought afar off. Thou hast beset me behind and before, and laid thine hand upon me. Such knowledge is too wonderful for me; it is high, I cannot attain unto it!" [1]

And it is one of the grandest, most significant facts in human history that, notwithstanding his intellectual limitations and superstitious fears, because he has maintained the altar of God as life's center of gravity, and never let die the consciousness that he was compassed about by the living God, the Oriental has been the channel of the sublimest spiritual revelation in the possession of man.

The histories of races are the records of their desires and rewards, of their seeking and finding. The law of compensation is all-embracing. In the long run "whatsoever a man soweth, that shall he also reap." [2] "He which soweth sparingly shall reap also sparingly; and he which soweth bountifully shall reap also bountifully." [3] In the material world the Oriental has sown but sparingly, and his harvests here have also been very meager. He has not achieved much in the world of science, industry, and commerce. As an industrial worker he has remained throughout his long history a user of hand tools. Previous to his very recent contact with the West, he never knew what structural iron and machinery were. As a merchant he has always been a

31

simple trader. He has never been a man of many inventions. His faithful repetition of the past has left no gulf between him and his remote ancestors. The implements and tools he uses to-day are like those his forefathers used in their day.

The supreme choice of the Oriental has been religion. To say that this choice has not been altogether a conscious one, that it has been the outcome of temperament, does by no means lessen its significance. From the beginning of his history on the earth to this day the Oriental has been conscious above all things of two supreme realities—God and the soul. What has always seemed to him to be his first and almost only duty was and is to form the most direct, most intimate connection between God and the soul. "The fear of the Lord," meaning most affectionate reverence, is to the son of the East not "the beginning of wisdom" as the English Bible has it, but the *height* or *acme* of wisdom. His first concern about his children is that they should know themselves as living souls, and God as their Creator and Father. An unbeliever in God has always been to the East a strange phenomenon. I never heard of atheism or of an atheist before I came in touch with Western culture in my native land.

My many years of intimate and sympathetic contact with the more varied, more intelligent life of the West has not tended in the least to lessen my reverence for religion nor to lower my regard for culture. Culture gives strength and symmetry to religious thought, and religion gives life and beauty to culture. And just as I believe that men should pray without ceasing, so also do I believe that they should strive to make their religious faith ever more free and more intelligent.

Yet the history of the Orient compels me to believe that the soil out of which scriptures spring is that whose life is the active sympathy of religion, regardless of the degree of acquired knowledge. When the depths of human nature are thoroughly saturated with this sympathy, then it is prepared both to receive and to give those thoughts of which scriptures are made. Industry and commerce have their good uses. But an industrial and commercialistic atmosphere is not conducive to the production of sacred books. Where the chief interests of life center in external things, religion is bound to become only one and perhaps a minor concern in life.

The Oriental has always lived in a world of spiritual mysteries. Fearful or confident, superstitious or rational, to him God has been all and in all. "The judgments of the Lord are true and righteous altogether. In keeping of them there is great reward." [4] The son of the East has been richly rewarded. He is the religious teacher of all mankind. Through him all scriptures have come into being. All the great, living religions of the world originated in Asia; and the three greatest of them—Judaism, Christianity, and Mohammedanism—have come into the world through the Semitic race in that little country called Syria. The perpetual yearning of the Oriental for spiritual dreams and visions has had its rewards. He sowed bountifully, he reaped bountifully.

Note the Syrian's daily language: it is essentially Biblical. He has no *secular* language. The only real break between his scriptures and the vocabulary of his daily life is that which exists between the classical and the vernacular. When you ask a Syrian about his business he will not answer, "We are doing well at present," but *"Allah mûn 'aim"* (God is giving bounteously). To one starting on a journey the phrase is not "Take good care of yourself," but "Go, in the keeping and protection of God." By example and precept we were trained from infancy in this manner of speech. Coming into a house, the visitor salutes by saying, "God grant you good morning," or "The peace of God come upon you." So it is written in the tenth chapter of Matthew, "And as ye enter into the house, salute it. And if the house be worthy, let your peace come upon it; but if it be not worthy, let your peace return unto you."

In saluting a day laborer at work we said, *"Allah, yaatik-el-afie"* (God give you health and strength). In saluting reapers in the field, or "gatherers of the increase" in the vineyards or olive groves, we said just the words of Boaz, in the second chapter of the Book of Ruth, when he "came from Bethlehem and said unto the reapers, The Lord be with you. And they answered him, The Lord bless thee." Or another Scriptural expression, now more extensively used on such occasions, "The blessing of the Lord be upon you!" It is to this custom that the withering imprecation which is recorded in the one hundred and twenty-ninth Psalm refers: "Let them all be confounded and turned back that hate Zion: let them be as the grass upon the housetops which withereth afore it groweth up: wherewith the mower filleth not his hand, nor he that bindeth sheaves his bosom. Neither do they which go by say, The blessing of the Lord be upon you: we bless you in the name of the Lord."

In asking a shepherd about his flock we said, "How are the blessed ones?" or a parent about his children, "How are the preserved ones?" They are preserved of God through their "angels," of whom the Master spoke when he said, "Take heed that ye despise not one of these little ones; for I say unto you that in heaven their angels do always behold the face of my Father." [5] Speaking of a good man we said, "The grace of God is poured upon his face." So in the Book of Proverbs, [6] "Blessings are upon the head of the just."

Akin to the foregoing are such expressions as these. In trying to rise from a sitting posture (the Syrians sit on the floor with their legs folded under them), a person, using the right arm for leverage, says, as he springs up, "Ya *Allah*" (O God [help]). In inquiring about the nature of an object, he says, "*Sho dinû?*" (what is its religion?) And one of the queerest expressions, when translated into English, is that employed to indicate that a kettleful of water, for example, has boiled beyond the required degree: "This water has turned to be an infidel" (*kaffer*). It may be noticed here that it is not the old theology only which associates the infidel with intense heat.

So this religious language is the Oriental's daily speech. I have stated in my autobiography that the men my father employed in his building operations were grouped according to their faith. He had so many Druses, so many Greek Orthodox, Maronites, and so forth.

The almost total abstinence from using "pious" language in ordinary business and social intercourse in America may be considered commendable in some ways, but I consider it a surrender of the soul to the body, a subordination of the spirit of the things which are eternal to the spirit of the things which are temporal. In my judgment, the superior culture of the West, instead of limiting the vocabulary of religion to the one hour of formal worship on Sunday, and scrupulously shunning it during the remainder of the week, should make its use, on a much higher plane than the Orient has yet discovered, coextensive with all the activities of life.

[1] Ps. cxxxix: 1-6.
[2] Gal. vi: 7.
[3] 2 Cor. ix: 6.
[4] Ps. xix: 9, 11.
[5] Matt. xviii: 10.
[6] x: 6.

Chapter Two - Imprecations

Again, the Oriental's consideration of life as being essentially religious makes him as pious in his imprecations and curses as he is in his aspirational prayer. Beyond all human intrigue, passion, and force, the great avenger is God. "Vengeance is mine, I will repay, saith the Lord." [1] "See now that I, even I, am he, and there is no God with me: I kill and I make alive; I wound and I heal; neither is there any that can deliver out of my hand." [2]

By priests and parents these precepts have been transmitted from generation to generation in the Orient, from time immemorial. We all were instructed in them by our elders with scrupulous care. Of course as weak mortals we always tried to avenge ourselves, and the idea of *thar* (revenge) lies deep in the Oriental nature. But to us our vengeance was nothing compared with what God did to our "ungodly" enemies and oppressors.

The Oriental's impetuosity and effusiveness make his imprecatory prayers, especially to the "unaccustomed ears" of Americans, blood-curdling. And I confess that on my last visit to Syria, my countrymen's (and especially my countrywomen's) bursts of pious wrath jarred heavily upon me. In his oral bombardment of his enemy the Oriental hurls such missiles as, "May God burn the bones of your fathers"; "May God exterminate your seed from the earth"; "May God cut off your supply of bread (*yakta rizkak*)"; "May you have nothing but the ground for a bed and the sky for covering"; "May your children be orphaned and your wife widowed"; and similar expressions.

Does not this sound exactly like the one hundred and ninth Psalm? Speaking of his enemy, the writer of that psalm says, "Let his days be few, and let another take his office. Let his children be fatherless, and his wife a widow. Let his children be continually vagabonds, and beg; let them seek their bread also out of their desolate places. Let there be none to extend mercy unto him; neither let there be any to favor his fatherless children. Let his posterity be cut off; and in the generation following let their name be blotted out."

The sad fact is that the Oriental has always considered his personal ene-mies to be the enemies of God also, and as such their end was destruction. Such sentiments mar the beauty of many of the Psalms. The enemies of the Israelites were considered the enemies of the God of Israel, and the enemies of a Syrian family are also the enemies of the patron saint of that family. In that most wonderful Scriptural passage—the one hundred and thirty-ninth Psalm—the singer cries, "Surely thou wilt slay the wicked, O God: depart from me, ye bloody men. For they speak against thee wickedly, and thine en-emies take thy name in vain. Do not I hate them, O Lord, that hate thee? and am I not grieved with those that rise against thee? *I hate them with perfect hatred: I count them mine enemies.*" Yet this ardent hater of his enemies most innocently turns to God and says in the next verse: "Search me, O God, and know my heart: try me and know my thoughts: *and see if there be any wicked way in me*, and lead me in the way everlasting."

This mixture of piety and hatred, uttered so naïvely and in good faith, is characteristically Syrian. Such were the mutual wishes I so often heard ex-pressed in our neighborhood and clan fights and quarrels in Syria. When so praying, the persons would beat upon their breasts and uncover their heads, as signs of the total surrender of their cause to an avenging Omnipotence. Of course the Syrians are not so cruel and heartless as such imprecations, espe-cially when cast in cold type, would lead one to believe. I am certain that if the little children of his enemy should become fatherless, the imprecator himself would be among the first to "favor" them. If you will keep in mind the juvenile temperament of the Oriental, already mentioned, and his habit of turning to God in all circumstances, as unreservedly as a child turns to his father, your judgment of the son of Palestine will be greatly tempered with mercy.

The one redeeming feature in these imprecatory petitions is that they have always served the Oriental as a safety-valve. Much of his wrath is vented in this manner. He is much more cruel in his words than in his deeds. As a rule the Orientals quarrel much, but fight little. By the time two antagonists have cursed and reviled each other so profusely they cool off, and thus graver con-sequences are averted. The Anglo-Saxon has outgrown such habits. In the first place the highly complex social order in which he lives calls for much more effective methods for the settling of disputes, and, in the second place, he has no time to waste on mere words. And just as the Anglo-Saxon smiles at the wordy fights of the Oriental, the Oriental shudders at the swiftness of the Anglo-Saxon in using his fists and his pistol. Both are needy of the grace of God.

[1] Rom. xii: 19. [2] Deut. xxxii: 39.

Chapter Three - Love of Enemies

The preceding chapter makes it very clear why Jesus opened the more profound depths of the spiritual life to his much-divided and almost hopelessly clannish countrymen, by commanding them to love their enemies. He who taught "as one having authority, and not as the scribes," knew the possibilities and powers of divine love as no man did. It is in such immortal precepts that we perceive his superiority to his time and people and the divinity of his character. His knowledge of the Father was so intimate and his repose in the Father's love so perfect that he could justly say, "I and my father are one."

"Ye have heard," he said to his followers, "that it hath been said, Thou shalt love thy neighbor [in the original, *quarib*—kinsman] and hate thine enemy: but I say unto you, love your enemies, bless them that curse you, do good to them that hate you, and pray for them which despitefully use you and persecute you; that ye may be the children of your father which is in heaven." [1]

Here we have the very heart and soul of the Gospel, and the dynamic power of Jesus' ministry of reconciliation. Yet to many devout Christians, as well as to unfriendly critics of the New Testament, the command, "Love your enemies," offers a serious perplexity. An "independent" preacher in a large Western city, after reading this portion of the Sermon on the Mount to his congregation, stated that Jesus' great discourse should be called, "The Sarcasm on the Mount." Is not love of enemies beyond the power of human nature?

This question is pertinent. And it is an obvious fact that we cannot love by command; we cannot love to order. This mysterious flow of soul which we call love is not of our own making; therefore we cannot *will* to love. Such a discussion, however, falls outside the scope of this publication. What I wish to offer here is a linguistic explanation which I believe will throw some light on this great commandment.

The word "love" has been more highly specialized in the West than in the East. In its proper English use it means only that ardent, amorous feeling which cannot be created by will and design. In the West the word "love" has been relieved of the function of expressing the less ardent desires such as the terms "to like," "to have good-will toward," and "to be well-disposed toward" imply.

Not so in the East. The word "like," meaning "to be favorably inclined toward," is not found either in the Bible or in the Arabic tongue. In the English version it is used in two places, but the translation is incorrect. In the twenty-fifth chapter of Deuteronomy the seventh verse, "If the man like not to take his brother's wife," should be rendered, "If the man *consent* not"; and in the fourth chapter of Amos, the fifth verse, "For this liketh you, O ye children of Israel," is in the original, "For this ye *loved*, O ye children of Israel." In any standard concordance of the Bible, the Hebrew verb *Aheb* (to love) precedes these quotations.

So to us Orientals the only word which can express any cordial inclination of approval is "love." One loves his wife and children, and loves grapes and figs and meat, if he likes these things. An employer says to an employee, "If you *love* to work for me according to this agreement, you can." It is nothing uncommon for one to say to a casual acquaintance whom he likes, "I must say, *Sahib* [friend], that I love you!" I know of no equivalent in the Arabic for the phrase, "I am interested in you." "Love" and "hate" are the usual terms by which to express approval and disapproval, as well as real love and hatred.

The Scriptural passages illustrative of this thought are not a few. In the ninth chapter of the Epistle to the Romans, the thirteenth verse, it is said, "As it is written, Jacob have I loved, but Esau have I hated." God does not "hate." The two terms here, "loved" and "hated," mean "approved" and "disapproved." It is as a father approves of the conduct of one of his children and disapproves that of another of them. Another example of this use of the word "hate" is found in the twenty-first chapter of Deuteronomy, the fifteenth verse: "If a man have two wives, one beloved, and another hated, and they have born him children, both the beloved and the hated; and if the firstborn son be hers that was hated: then it shall be, when he maketh his sons to inherit that which he hath, that he may not make the son of the beloved firstborn before the son of the hated, which is indeed the first-born: but he shall acknowledge the son of the hated for the firstborn, by giving him a double portion of all that he hath." Here it is safe to infer that the writer meant to distinguish between the wife who was a "favorite" and the one who was not. There could be no valid reason why a husband should live with a wife whom he really hated when he could very easily divorce her, according to the Jewish law, and marry another. In such a case the husband was simply partial in his love. The hatred which is felt toward an enemy and a destroyer does not apply here.

Another Scriptural passage which illustrates the free use of the word "love" is the story of the rich man in the tenth chapter of St. Mark's Gospel. Beginning with the seventeenth verse, the passage reads: "And when he was gone forth into the way, there came one running, and kneeling to him, and asked him, Good Master, what shall I do that I may inherit eternal life? And Jesus said unto him, Why callest thou me good? there is none good but one, that is, God. Thou knowest the commandments, Do not commit adultery, Do not kill, Do not steal, Do not bear false witness, Defraud not, Honor thy father and mother. And he answered and said unto him, Master, all these have I observed from my youth. *Then Jesus, beholding him, loved him*, and said unto him, One thing thou lackest"; and so forth. Apparently the brief conversation with the young man showed Jesus that his questioner was both polite and intelligent, so the Master liked him. Stating the case in Western phraseology it may be said that the young Hebrew seeker was an agreeable, or likable man.

37

Quite different is the import of the word "love" in such of the Master's sayings as are found in the fifteenth chapter of St. John's Gospel: "As the Father hath loved me, so have I loved you: continue ye in my love. This is my commandment, That ye love one another, as I have loved you." Here the term "love" is used in its truest and purest sense.

From all this it may be seen that when the Great Oriental Teacher said to his countrymen, who considered all other clans than their own as their enemies, "Love your enemies," he did not mean that they should be enamored of them, but that they should have good will toward them. We cannot love by will and design, but we certainly can will to be well disposed even toward those who, we believe, have ill will toward us. He who really thinks this an impossibility gives evidence not of superior "critical knowledge," but of being still in the lower stages of human evolution.

But I have something more to say on this great subject. Whether used in a general or a highly specialized sense the word "Love" speaks indeed of the "greatest thing in the world."

When the Master of the Art of Living said, "Love your enemies," he urged upon the minds of men the divinest law of human progress. Yet compliance with this demand seems, to the majority of men, to be beyond the reach of humanity. When you are admonished to love your enemies, you will be likely to think of the meanest, most disagreeable human being you know and wonder as to how you are going to love *such* a person. But the Master's law far transcends this narrow conception of love. Its deeper meaning, when understood, renders such a conception shallow and childish. It is to be found, not in the freakish moods of the sensibility, but in the realm of permanent ideals.

There are in the world two forces at work, love and hatred. Hatred destroys, love builds; hatred injures, love heals; hatred embitters life, love sweetens it; hatred is godlessness, love is godliness. The supreme question, therefore, is, not as to whether there are unlovable persons in the world or not, but rather, which one of these two forces would you have to rule your own life and the life of humanity at large, love or hatred? Which nutrition would you give your own soul and the souls of those who are near and dear to you, that of hatred, or that of love? Can it be your aim in life to aid that power which injures, destroys, embitters life and estranges from God, or the power which heals, builds up, sweetens life and makes one with God?

You say you have been injured through the malicious designs of others, you are pained by the injury, and a sense of hatred impels you to avenge yourself. But what formed such designs against you, love or hatred? Hatred! You enjoy, idealize, adore the love of those who love you. The designs of love give you joyous satisfaction, and not pain. You know now by actual personal experience that the fruits of hatred are bitter, and the fruits of love are sweet. Is it your duty, therefore, to give your life over to the power of hatred, and thus increase its dominion among men and multiply its bitter, poisonous fruit in the world, or to consecrate your life to the power of love, which you idealize and adore, and whose fruits are joy and peace?

This, therefore, is the Master's law of love: Give your life and service to that power which merits your holiest regard and engages your purest affections, regardless of the "evil and the undeserving." Recognize no enemies, and you shall have none. The only power which can defeat the designs of hatred is love. The foams of hatred and fumes of vengeance are destined to pass away with all their possessors; only love is permanent and sovereign good.

The man of hatred is destined, sooner or later, to lose his nobler qualities, his own self-respect and the respect of others, and to occupy the smallest and most undesirable social sphere. Therefore love, and do not hate! Exercise good will toward those even who have injured you.

You may not be able to reach and redeem by your generous thoughts and designs such persons as have injured you, but a hundred others may learn from you the law of redeeming love. Let your children grow to know you as a man of love. Let your employees and fellow citizens think of you as a man of peace and good will, a builder and not a destroyer. Let your fireside be ever cheered by the music of love. When the shadows of night fall and you come to enter into the unknown land of sleep, let loving thoughts be your companions; let them course into the deepest recesses of your nature and leaven your entire being. Be a man of love! Love even your blind and misguided enemies!

[1] Matt. v: 43-45.

Chapter Four - "The Unveracious Oriental"

The Oriental's juvenile temperament and his partial disregard for concrete facts have led his Anglo-Saxon cousin to consider him as essentially unveracious. "You cannot believe what an Oriental says." "The Orientals are the children of the 'Father of Lies.'" "Whatever an Oriental says, the opposite is likely to be the truth"; and so forth.

I do not wish in the least to undertake to excuse or even condone the Oriental's unveracity, any more than to approve of the ethics of American politicians during a political campaign. I have no doubt that the Oriental suffers more from the universal affliction of untruthfulness than does the Anglo-Saxon, and that he sorely needs to restrict his fancy, and to train his intellect to have more respect for facts. Nevertheless, I feel compelled to say that a clear understanding of some of the Oriental's modes of thought will quash many of the indictments against his veracity. His ways will remain different from the ways of the Anglo-Saxon, and perhaps not wholly agreeable to the latter; but the son of the East—the dreamer and writer of scriptures—will be credited with more honesty of purpose.

It is unpleasant to an Anglo-Saxon to note how many things an Oriental says, but does not mean. And it is distressing to an Oriental to note how many things the Anglo-Saxon means, but does not say. To an unreconstructed Syrian the brevity, yea, even curtness, of an Englishman or an American, seems to sap life of its pleasures and to place a disproportionate value on time. For the Oriental, the primary value of time must not be computed in terms of business and money, but in terms of sociability and good fellowship. Poetry, and not prosaic accuracy, must be the dominant feature of speech.

There is much more of intellectual inaccuracy than of moral delinquency in the Easterner's speech. His misstatements are more often the result of indifference than the deliberate purpose to deceive. One of his besetting sins is his *ma besay-il*—it does not matter. He sees no essential difference between nine o'clock and half after nine, or whether a conversation took plate on the housetop or in the house. The main thing is to know the substance of what happened, with as many of the supporting details as may be conveniently remembered. A case may be overstated or understated, not necessarily for the purpose of deceiving, but to impress the hearer with the significance or the insignificance of it. If a sleeper who had been expected to rise at sunrise should oversleep and need to be awakened, say half an hour or an hour later than the appointed time, he is then aroused with the call, "Arise, it is noon already—*qûm sar edh-hir*." Of a strong and brave man it is said, "He can split the earth—*yekkid elaridh*." The Syrians suffer from no misunderstanding in such cases. They *discern* one another's meaning.

So also many Scriptural passages need to be *discerned*. The purpose of the Oriental speaker or writer must be sought often beyond the letter of his statement, which he uses with great freedom.

In the first chapter of St. Mark's Gospel, the thirty-second and thirty-third verses, it is said, "And at even, when the sun did set, they brought unto him all that were diseased, and them that were possessed of devils. And *all the city* was gathered together at the door." The swiftness with which the poor people in Eastern communities bring their sick to a healer, be he a prophet or only a physician, is proverbial. Because of the scarcity of physicians, as well as of money with which to pay for medical attendance, when a healer is summoned to a home many afflicted persons come or are brought to him. The peoples of the East have always believed also in the healing of diseases by religious means. When a prophet arises the first thing expected of him is that he should heal the sick. Both the priest and the physician are appealed to in time of trouble. To those who followed and believed in him Jesus was the healer of both the soul and the body. But note the account of the incident before us. The place was the city of Capernaum, and we are told that "*all the city* was gathered together at the door" of the house where Jesus was bestowing the loving, healing touch upon the sick. Was the *whole city* at the door? Were *all* the sick in that large city brought into that house for Jesus to heal them? Here we are confronted by a physical impossibility. An Anglo-Saxon chronicler would have said, "Quite a number gathered at the door," which in all probability would have been a *correct* report.

But to the Oriental writer the object of the report was not *to determine the number* of those who stood outside, nor to insist that each and every sick person in Capernaum was brought into the humble home of Simon and Andrew. It was rather to glorify the Great Teacher and his divine work of mercy, and not to give a photographic report of the attendant circumstances. The saying, "Quite a number gathered at the door," may be correct, but to an Oriental it is absolutely colorless and tasteless, an inexcusably parsimonious use of the imagination.

Take another Scriptural passage. In the seventeenth chapter of St. Matthew's Gospel, the first verse, we read: "And after six days Jesus taketh Peter, James, and John his brother, and bringeth them up into an high mountain apart, and was transfigured before them; and his face did shine as the sun." "After six days" from what time? In the preceding chapter a general reference to time is made in the thirteenth verse, where it is said: "When Jesus came into the coasts of Cæsarea Philippi, he asked his disciples, saying, Whom do men say that I the Son of man am?" But here no definite date is given. Chapter sixteenth ends with those great words, "For whosoever will save his life shall lose it: and whosoever will lose his life for my sake shall find it. For what is a man profited, if he shall gain the whole world, and lose his own soul?" The two last verses of this chapter promise the speedy coming of the Kingdom.

"After six days" from what time? Well, what does it matter from what time? Do you not see that the object of the record is to give a glimpse of what happened on that "high mountain" where the light and glory of the unseen world were reflected in the face of the Christ?

The intelligent lay reader of the New Testament cannot fail to notice, especially in the Gospels, gaps and abrupt beginnings such as "In those days"; "Then came the disciples to Jesus"; "And it came to pass"; and many similar expressions which seem to point nowhere. The record seems to be rather incoherent. Yes, such difficulties, which are due largely to the Oriental's indifference to little details, exist in the Bible, but they are very unimportant. The central purpose of these books is to enable the reader to perceive the secret of a holy personality, whose mission was, is, and forever shall be, to emancipate the soul of man from the bondage of a world of fear, weakness, sin, and doubt, and lead it onward and upward to the realms of faith, hope, and love. This purpose the Scriptures abundantly subserve.

Chapter Five - Impressions *vs.* Literal Accuracy

A Syrian's chief purpose in a conversation is to convey an impression by whatever suitable means, and not to deliver his message in scientifically accurate terms. He expects to be judged not by what he *says*, but by what he *means*. He does not expect his hearer to listen to him with the quizzical courtesy of a "cool-headed Yankee," and to interrupt the flow of conversation by saying, with the least possible show of emotion, "Do I understand you to say," etc. No; he piles up his metaphors and superlatives, reinforced by a theatrical display of gestures and facial expressions, in order to make the hearer *feel* his meaning.

The Oriental's speech is always "illustrated." He speaks as it were in pictures. With him the spoken language goes hand in hand with the more ancient gesture language. His profuse gesticulation is that phase of his life which first challenges the attention of Occidental travelers in the East. He points to almost everything he mentions in his speech, and would portray every feeling and emotion by means of some bodily movement. No sooner does he mention his eye than his index finger points to or even touches that organ. "Do you understand me?" is said to an auditor with the speaker's finger on his own temple. In rebuking one who makes unreasonable demands upon him, a Syrian would be likely to stoop down and say, "Don't you want to ride on my back?"

One of the most striking examples of this manner of speech in the Bible is found in the twenty-first chapter of the Book of Acts. Beginning with the tenth verse, the writer says: "And as we tarried there [at Cæsarea] many days, there came down from Judea a certain prophet, named Agabus. And when he was come unto us, he took Paul's girdle, and bound his own hands and feet, and said, Thus saith the Holy Ghost, So shall the Jews at Jerusalem bind the man that owneth this girdle, and shall deliver him into the hands of the Gentiles." Now an Occidental teacher would not have gone into all that trouble. He would have said to the great apostle, "Now you understand I don't mean to interfere with your business, but if I were you I would n't go down to Jerusalem. Those Jews there are not pleased with what you are doing, and would be likely to make things unpleasant for you." But in all probability such a polite hint would not have made Paul's companions weep, nor caused him to say, "What mean ye to weep and to break mine heart? for I am ready not to be bound only, but also to die at Jerusalem for the name of the Lord Jesus."

It is also because the Syrian loves to speak in pictures, and to subordinate literal accuracy to the total impression of an utterance, that he makes such extensive use of figurative language. Instead of saying to the Pharisees, "Your pretensions to virtue and good birth far exceed your actual practice of virtue," John the Baptist cried: "O generation of vipers, who hath warned you to flee from the wrath to come? Bring forth, therefore, fruits meet for repentance: and think not to say within yourselves, We have Abraham to our father: for I say unto you that God is able *of these stones* to raise up children unto Abraham."

Just as the Oriental loves to flavor his food strongly and to dress in bright colors, so is he fond of metaphor, exaggeration, and positiveness in speech. To him mild accuracy is weakness. A host of illustrations of this thought rise in my mind as I recall my early experiences as a Syrian youth. I remember how those jovial men who came to our house to "sit"—that is, to make a call of indefinite duration—would make their wild assertions and back them up by vows which they never intended to keep. The one would say, "What I say to you is the truth, and if it is not, I will cut off my right arm"—grasping it—"at the shoulder." "I promise you this,"—whatever the promise might be,—"and if I fail in fulfilling my promise I will pluck out my right eye."

To such speech we always listened admiringly and respectfully. But we never had the remotest idea that in any circumstances the speaker would carry out his resolution, or that his hearers had a right to demand it from him. He simply was in earnest; or as an American would say, "He meant that he was right."

Such an Oriental mode of thought furnishes us with the background for Jesus' saying, "If thy right eye offend thee, pluck it out, and cast it from thee. If thy right hand offend thee, cut it off, and cast it from thee." [1]

To many Western Christians, especially in the light of the Protestant doctrine of the infallibility of the letter of the Bible, these sayings of Christ present insurmountable difficulties. To such the question, "How can I be a true disciple of Christ, if I do not obey what he commands?" makes these misunderstood sayings of Christ great stumbling blocks. Some time ago a lady wrote me a letter saying that at a prayer-meeting which she attended, the minister, after reading the fifth chapter of Matthew, which contains these commands, said, "If we are true Christians we must not shrink from obeying these explicit commands of our Lord."

My informant stated also that on hearing that, she asked the preacher, "Suppose the tongue should offend, and we should cut it off; should we be better Christians than if we did endeavor to atone for the offense in some other way?" The preacher, after a moment of perplexed silence, said, "If there is no one here who can answer this question, we will sing a hymn."

The best commentary on these sayings of Christ is given by Paul in the sixth chapter of his Epistle to the Romans. This is precisely what the Master meant: "Neither yield ye your members as instruments of unrighteousness unto sin; but yield yourselves unto God, as those that are alive from the dead, and your members as instruments of righteousness unto God." Cutting or mutilation of the body has nothing to do with either passage, nor indeed with the Christian life. The amputation of an arm that steals is no sure guaranty of the removal of the desire to steal; nor would the plucking out of a lustful eye do away with the lust which uses the eye for an instrument.

With this should be classed also the following commands: "Whosoever shall smite thee on the right cheek, turn to him the other also." "If any man will sue thee at the law, and take away thy coat, let him have thy cloak also; and whosoever shall compel thee to go a mile, go with him twain." [2]

The command to give the coat and the cloak to a disputant, rather than to go to law with him, will seem much more perplexing when it is understood that these words mean the "under garment" and the "upper garment." The Orientals are not in the habit of wearing a coat and a cloak or overcoat. In the Arabic version we have the *thaub* ("th" as in "throw") and the *rada'*. The *thaub* is the main article of clothing—the ample gown worn over a shirt next to the body. The *rada'* is the cloak worn on occasions over the *thaub*.

43

The Scriptural command literally is, "To one who would quarrel with thee and would take thy *thaub*, give him the *rada'* also." It may be clearly seen here that literal compliance with this admonition would leave the non-resistant person, so far as clothes are concerned, in a pitiable condition.

The concluding portion of this paragraph in the fifth chapter of St. Matthew's Gospel—the forty-second verse—presents another difficulty. It says, "Give to him that asketh thee, and from him that would borrow of thee turn not thou away." Of all those whom I have heard speak disparagingly of this passage I particularly recall a lawyer, whom I knew in a Western State, whose dislike for these words of Christ amounted almost to a mental affliction. It seems to me that on every single occasion when he and I discussed the Scriptures together, or spoke of Christianity, I found him armed with this passage as his most effective weapon against the innocent Nazarene. "What was Jesus thinking of," he would say, "when he uttered these words? What would become of our business interests and financial institutions if we gave to every one that asked of us, and lent money without good security to every Tom, Dick, and Harry?"

The thought involved in this text suffers from the unconditional manner in which it is presented, and which gives it its Oriental flavor. Seeing that he was addressing those who knew what he meant, the writer did not deem it necessary to state exactly the reason why this command was given. It seems, however, that when Jesus spoke those words he had in mind the following passage: "And if thy brother be waxed poor, and his hand fail with thee; then thou shalt uphold him: as a stranger and a sojourner shall he live with thee. Take thou no interest of him or increase, but fear thy God: that thy brother may live with thee. *Thou shalt not give him thy money upon interest*, nor give him thy victuals for increase." [3] According to this legal stipulation, an Israelite could not lawfully charge a fellow Israelite interest on a loan. Therefore, "as a matter of business," the money-lenders preferred to lend their money to the Gentiles, from whom they were permitted to take interest, and to "turn away" from borrowers of their own race. And as the teachers of Israel of his day often assailed Jesus for his non-observance of the law, he in turn never failed to remind them of the fact that their own practices did greater violence to the law than his own liberal interpretation of it in the interest of man.

From all that I know of Oriental modes of thought and life I cannot conceive that Jesus meant by all these sayings to give brute force the right of way in human life. He himself drove the traders out of the temple by physical force. These precepts were not meant to prohibit the use of force in self-defense and for the protection of property, but were given as an antidote to that relentless law of revenge which required "an eye for an eye and a tooth for a tooth." The Master does not preach a gospel of helplessness, but enjoins a manly attitude toward peace and concord, in place of a constantly active desire for vengeance and strife.

Again let me say that an Oriental expects to be judged chiefly by what he means and not by what he says. As a rule, the Oriental is not altogether unaware of the fact that, as regards the letter, his statements are often sadly lacking in correctness. But I venture to say that when a person who is conversing with me knows that I know that what he is saying is not exactly true I may not like his manner of speech, yet I cannot justly call him a liar.

A neighbor of mine in a Mount Lebanon village makes a trip to Damascus and comes to my house of an evening to tell me all about it. He would not be a Syrian if he did not give wings to his fancy and present me with an idealistic painting of his adventure, instead of handing me a photograph. I listen and laugh and wonder. I know his statements are not wholly correct, and he knows exactly how I feel about it. We both are aware, however, that the proceedings of the evening are not those of a business transaction, but of an entertainment. My friend does not maliciously misrepresent the facts; he simply loves to speak in poetic terms and is somewhat inhospitable to cross-examination. Certainly we would not buy and sell sheep and oxen and fields and vineyards after that fashion, but we like to be so entertained. Beyond the wide margin of social hospitality and the latitude of intellectual tolerance, I am aware of the fact that in all the flourish of metaphor and simile, what my visitor really meant to say was either that his trip to Damascus was pleasant or that it was hazardous, and that there were many interesting things to see in that portion of the world; all of which was indubitably true.

While on a visit to Syria, after having spent several years in this country, where I had lived almost exclusively with Americans, I was very strongly impressed by the decidedly sharp contrast between the Syrian and the American modes of thought. The years had worked many changes in me, and I had become addicted to the more compact phraseology of the American social code.

In welcoming me to his house, an old friend of mine spoke with impressive cheerfulness as follows: "You have extremely honored me by coming into my abode [*menzel*], I am not worthy of it. This house is yours; you can burn it if you wish. My children also are at your disposal; I would sacrifice them all for your pleasure. What a blessed day this is, now that the light of your countenance has shone upon us"; and so forth, and so on.

I understood my friend fully and most agreeably, although it was not easy for me to translate his words to my American wife without causing her to be greatly alarmed at the possibility that the house would be set on fire and the children slain for our pleasure. What my friend really meant in his effusive welcome was no more or less than what a gracious American host means when he says, "I am delighted to see you; please make yourself at home."

Had the creed-makers of Christendom approached the Bible by way of Oriental psychology, had they viewed the Scriptures against the background of Syrian life, they would not have dealt with Holy Writ as a jurist deals with legislative enactments. Again, had the unfriendly critics of the Bible real acquaintance with the land of its birth, they would not have been so sure that the Bible was "a mass of impossibilities." The sad fact is that the Bible has suffered violence from literalists among its friends, as from its enemies.

45

For example, in their failure to heal a sick lad [4] the disciples came to Jesus and asked him why they could not do the beneficent deed. According to the Revised and the Arabic versions, the Master answered, "Because of your unbelief; for verily I say unto you, If ye have faith as a grain of mustard seed, ye shall say unto this mountain, Remove hence to yonder place, and it shall remove." Colonel Robert Ingersoll never tired of challenging the Christians of America to put this scripture to a successful test, and thus *convince* him that the Bible is inspired. In the face of such a challenge the "believer" is likely to feel compelled to admit that the church does not have the required amount of faith, else it could remove mountains.

To one well acquainted with the Oriental manner of speech this saying was not meant to fix a rule of conduct, but to idealize faith. In order to do this in real Syrian fashion, Jesus spoke of an infinitesimal amount of faith as being capable of moving the biggest object on earth. His disciples must have understood him clearly, because we have no record that they ever tried to remove mountains by faith and prayer. It would be most astounding, indeed, if Christ really thought that those disciples, who forsook all and followed him, had not as much faith as a grain of mustard seed, and yet said to them, "Ye are the light of the world. Ye are the salt of the earth."

Of a similar character is the Master's saying, "It is easier for a camel to go through the eye of a needle, than for a rich man to enter into the kingdom of God," [5] which has quickened the exegetical genius of commentators to mighty efforts in "expounding the Scriptures." Judging by the vast number of persons in this country who have asked my opinion, as a Syrian, concerning its correctness, and the fact that I have myself seen it in print, the following interpretation of this passage must have been much in vogue.

The walled cities and feudal castles of Palestine, the explanation runs, have large gates. Because of their great size, such gates are opened only on special occasions to admit chariots and caravans. Therefore, in order to give pedestrians thoroughfare, a smaller opening about the size of an ordinary door is made in the center of the great gate, near to the ground. Now this smaller door through which a camel cannot pass is the eye of the needle mentioned in the Gospel.

I once heard a Sunday-School superintendent explain this passage to his scholars by saying that a camel could pass through this eye of a needle— meaning the door—if he was not loaded. Therefore, and by analogy, if we cast off our load of sin outside, we can easily enter into the kingdom of heaven.

Were the camel and the gate left out, this statement would be an excellent fatherly admonition. There is perhaps no gate in the celestial city large enough to admit a man with a load of sin strapped to his soul. However, the chief trouble with these explanations of the "eye-of-the-needle" passage is that they are wholly untrue.

This saying is current in the East, and in all probability it was a common saying there long before the advent of Christ. But I never knew that small

46

door in a city or a castle gate to be called the needle's eye; nor indeed the large gate to be called the needle. The name of that door, in the common speech of the country, is the "plum," and I am certain the Scriptural passage makes no reference to it whatever.

The Koran makes use of this expression in one of its purest classical Arabic passages. The term employed here—*sûm-el-khiat*—can mean only the sewing instrument, and nothing else.

Nothing can show more clearly the genuine Oriental character of this New Testament passage and that of the Teacher who uttered it, than the intense positiveness of its thought and the unrestrained flight of its imagery. I can just hear the Master say it. Jesus' purpose was to state that it was extremely difficult "for them that trust in riches to enter into the Kingdom of God." [6] To this end he chose the biggest animal and the smallest opening known to his people and compared the impossibility of a camel passing through the eye of a needle with that of a man weighted down with earthly things becoming one with God.

The Master's rebuke of the scribes and pharisees, "Ye blind guides, which strain at a gnat and swallow a camel," [7] expresses a similar thought in a different form and connection. There is no need here to puzzle over the anatomical problem as to whether the throat of a Pharisee was capacious enough to gulp a camel down. The strong and agreeable Oriental flavor of this saying comes from the sharp contrast between the size of the gnat and that of the camel. So the Master employed it in order to show the glaring contradictions in the precepts and practices of the priests of his day, who tithed mint and rue, but "passed over judgment and the love of God."

One of the most interesting examples of Oriental speech is found in the eighteenth chapter of St. Matthew's Gospel, the twenty-first verse: "Then came Peter and said to him, Lord how oft shall my brother sin against me, and I forgive him? till seven times? Jesus saith unto him, I say not unto thee, until seven times; but, until seventy times seven." Did Jesus really mean that an offender should be forgiven four hundred and ninety times? Would it be to the interest of the offender himself and to society at large to forgive an embezzler, a slanderer or a prevaricator four hundred and ninety times? Is not punishment which is guided by reason and sympathy, and whose end is corrective, really a great aid in character-building? Let us try to interpret this passage with reference to certain scenes in Jesus' own life. In the sixteenth chapter of Matthew, the twenty-first verse, we read: "From that time forth began Jesus to show unto his disciples, how that he must go unto Jerusalem, and suffer many things of the elders and chief priests and scribes, and be killed, and be raised again the third day. Then Peter took him, and began to rebuke him, saying, Lord: this shall not be unto thee. But he turned, and said unto Peter, *Get thee behind me, Satan: thou art an offence to me*: for thou savourest not the things that be of God, but those that be of men."

In the second chapter of St. John's Gospel, the thirteenth verse, we are told: "And the Jews' passover was at hand, and Jesus went up to Jerusalem, and found in the temple those that sold oxen and sheep and doves, and the changers of money sitting: *and when he had made a scourge of small cords, he drove them all out of the temple*, and the sheep, and the oxen; and poured out the changers' money, and overthrew the tables; and said unto them that sold doves, Take these things hence; make not my Father's house an house of merchandise."

The forgiving "seventy times seven" did not apply, as it seems, in these cases. In the very chapter from which this saying comes, [8] the Master gives us two superb examples of certain and somewhat swift retribution for offenses. In the fifteenth verse, he says: "Moreover, if thy brother shall trespass against thee, go tell him his fault between thee and him alone: if he shall hear thee, thou hast gained thy brother. But if he will not hear thee, then take with thee one or two more, that in the mouth of two or three witnesses every word may be established. And if he neglect to hear them, tell it unto the church; but if he neglect to hear the church, *let him be unto thee as an heathen man and a publican.*"

The parable of the "certain king" and the "wicked servant" follows immediately the "seventy times seven" passage. "Therefore is the kingdom of heaven likened unto a certain king, which would take account of his servants. And when he had begun to reckon, one was brought unto him, which owed him ten thousand talents. But forasmuch as he had not to pay, his lord commanded him to be sold, and his wife, and children, and all that he had, and payment be made. The servant therefore fell down and worshipped him, saying, Lord, have patience with me, and I will pay thee all. Then the Lord of that servant was moved with compassion, and loosed him, and forgave him the debt. But the same servant went out, and found one of his fellowservants, which owed him an hundred pence: and he laid hands on him, and took him by the throat, saying, Pay me that thou owest. And his fellowservant fell down at his feet, and besought him, saying, Have patience with me, and I will pay thee all. And he would not: but went and cast him into prison, till he should pay the debt. So when his fellowservants saw what was done, they were very sorry, and came and told unto their lord all that was done. Then his lord, after that he had called him, said unto him, O thou wicked servant, I forgave thee all that debt, because thou desiredst me: shouldest not thou also have had compassion on thy fellow-servant, even as I had pity on thee? *And his lord was wroth, and delivered him to the tormentors, till he should pay all that was due unto him.* So likewise shall my heavenly Father do also unto you, if ye from your hearts forgive not every one his brother their trespasses."

Now as a matter of fact the lord of the wicked servant did not forgive him seventy times seven, but "delivered him to the tormentors" for his first offense. Will the heavenly Father do *likewise*? Do we not have irreconcilable contradictions in these Scriptural passages?

No doubt there are difficulties here. But once the "seventy-times-seven" passage is clearly understood, the difficulties will, I believe, disappear. In harmony with his legalistic preconception, Peter chose the full and sacred number "seven" as a very liberal measure of forgiveness. Apparently Jesus' purpose was to make forgiveness a matter of disposition, sympathy, and discretion, rather than of arithmetic. To this end he made use of an Oriental saying which meant *indefiniteness*, rather than a fixed rule. This saying occurs in one of the most ancient Old Testament narratives, and, most fittingly, in a bit of poetry: [9]

"And Lamech said unto his wives:
Adah and Zillah, hear my voice;
Ye wives of Lamech, hearken unto my speech:
For I have slain a man for wounding me,
And a young man for bruising me:
If Cain shall be avenged sevenfold
Truly Lamech seventy and sevenfold."

In both Testaments the meaning of the saying is the same—indefiniteness. It is one of that host of Bible passages and current Oriental sayings which must be judged by what they *mean*, and not by what they *say*. The writer of the eighteenth chapter of Matthew grouped those seemingly contradictory passages together, because they all dealt with forgiveness. That they must have been spoken under various circumstances is very obvious. The object of the admonition concerning the trespassing brother (verses 15-17) is to encourage Christians to "reason together" in a fraternal spirit about the differences which may arise between them, and, *if at all possible*, to win the offending member back to the fold. And the object of the parable of the "wicked servant" is to contrast the spirit of kindness with that of cruelty.

[1] Matt. v: 29-30.
[2] Matt. v: 39-41.
[3] Lev. xxv: 35; Revised Version.
[4] Matt. xvii: 19.
[5] Matt. xix: 24.

[6] Mark x: 24.
[7] Matt. xxiii: 24.
[8] Matt. xviii.
[9] Gen. iv: 23; Revised Version.

Chapter Six - Speaking in Parables

Teaching and conversing in parables and proverbs is a distinctly Oriental characteristic. A parable is a word picture whose purpose is not to construct a definition or to establish a doctrine, but to convey an impression. However, the Oriental makes no distinction between a proverb and a parable. In both the Hebrew and the Arabic, the word *mathel* signifies either a short wise saying, such as may be found in the Book of Proverbs, or a longer utterance, such as a New Testament parable. In the Arabic Bible, the wise sayings of the Book of Proverbs are called *amthal*, and the parabolic discourses of Jesus are also called *amthal*. This term is the plural of *mathel* (parable or proverb). This designation includes also any wise poetical saying, or any human state of fortune or adversity. Thus a very generous man becomes a *mathel bilkaram* (a parable of generosity); and a man of unsavory reputation becomes a *mathel beinennass* (a saying or a by-word among the people). In the forty-fourth Psalm, the fourteenth verse, the poet cries: "Thou makest us a by-word among the nations, a shaking of the head among the people." A fine illustration of the *mathel* as a poetical saying, although not strictly allegorical, is the opening passage of the twenty-ninth chapter of the Book of Job, where it is said:—

"And Job again took up his parable and said,
Oh that I were as in the months of old,
As in the days when God watched over me;
When his lamp shined upon my head,
And by his light I walked through darkness;
As I was in the ripeness of my days,
When the friendship of God was upon my tent;
When the Almighty was yet with me,
And my children were about me;
When my steps were washed with butter,
And the rock poured me out rivers of oil!" [1]

Where in human literature can we find a passage to surpass in beauty and tenderness this introspective utterance?

Parabolic speech is dear to the Oriental heart. It is poetical, mystical, sociable. In showing the reason why Jesus taught in parables, Biblical writers speak of the indirect method, the picture language, the concealing of the truth from those "who had not the understanding," and so forth. But those writers fail to mention a most important reason, namely, the *sociable* nature of such a method of teaching, which is so dear to the Syrian heart. In view of the small value the Orientals place upon time, the story-teller, the speaker in parables, is to them the most charming conversationalist. Why be so prosy, brief, and abstract? The spectacular charm and intense concreteness of the parable of the Prodigal Son is infinitely more agreeable to the Oriental mind than the general precept that God will forgive his truly penitent children. How romantic and how enchanting to me are the memories of those *sehrat* (evening gatherings) at my father's house! How simple and how human was the homely wisdom of the stories and the parables which were spoken on those occasions. The elderly men of the clan loved to speak of what "was said in the ancient days" (*qadeem ezzeman*). "*Qal el-wathel*" (said the parable) prefaced almost every utterance. And as the speaker proceeded to relate a parable and to reinforce the ancient saying by what his own poetic fancy could create at the time of kindred material, we listened admiringly, and looked forward with ecstatic expectation to the *maana* (meaning, or moral). Oral traditions, the Scriptures, Mohammedan literature, and other rich sources are drawn upon, both for instruction in wisdom and for entertainment.

In picturing the condition of one who has been demoralized beyond redemption, the entertaining speaker proceeds in this fashion: "Once upon a time a certain man fell from the housetop and was badly injured. The neighbors came and carried him into the house and placed him in bed. Then one of his friends approached near to the injured man and said to him, 'Asaad, my beloved friend, how is your condition [*kief halak*]?' The much-pained man opened his mouth and said, 'My two arms are broken; my back and one of my legs are broken; one of my eyes is put out; I am badly wounded in the breast, and feel that my liver is severed. But I trust that God will restore me.' Whereupon his friend answered, 'Asaad, I am distressed. But if this is your condition, it will be much easier for God to make a new man to take your place than to restore you!'"

One of the most beautiful parables I know, and which I often heard my father relate, bears on the subject of partiality, and is as follows:—

"Once upon a time there were two men, the one named Ibrahim, the other Yusuf. Each of the men had a camel. It came to pass that when Yusuf fell sick he asked of his neighbor Ibrahim, who was about to journey to Alappo, to take his camel with him also, with a load of merchandise. Yusuf begged Ibrahim to treat the camel in exactly the same manner as he did his own, and promised him that if God kept him alive until he came back he would repay him both the good deed, and the cost of the camel's keep. Ibrahim accepted the trust, and took his journey to Alappo, with the two camels. Upon his return Yusuf saw that his own camel did not look so well as Ibrahim's. So he spoke to his friend: 'Ibrahim, by the life of God, what has happened to my camel? He is not as good as your camel. O Ibrahim, did you care for my camel as you did for your camel?' Then Ibrahim answered and said, 'By the life of God, O Yusuf, I fed, and watered, and groomed your camel as I did my camel. God witnesseth between us, Yusuf, this is the truth. But I will say to you, you my eyes, my heart, that when night came and I lay me down on my cloak to sleep between the two camels, I placed my head nearer to my camel than to yours.'"

It was the desirableness to Orientals of this type of speech which prompted the writer of the Gospel of Matthew to say of Jesus, "And without a parable spake he not unto them." [2] This utterance itself is characteristically Oriental. As a matter of fact, Jesus *did* often speak to the multitude *without* parables. But his strong tendency to make use of the parable, and its agreeableness to his hearers, seemed to the Scriptural writer to be a sufficient justification for his sweeping assertion.

Of the New Testament parables some are quoted in this work in connection with other subjects than that with which this chapter deals. I will mention here a few more of these sayings as additional illustrations of the present subject, and with reference to the allusions to Oriental life which they contain.

In the thirteenth chapter of Matthew, we have the parable of the wheat and the tares: "The kingdom of heaven is likened unto a man which sowed good seed in his field: but while men slept, his enemy came and sowed tares among the wheat, and went his way. But when the blade was sprung up, and brought forth fruit, then appeared the tares also."

The tare (*zewan*) is a grain which when ground with the wheat and eaten causes dizziness and nausea, a state much like seasickness. For this reason this plant is hated by the Syrians, although they use tares very extensively as chicken feed. Wheat merchants are likely to sell *kameh mizwen* (wheat mixed with tares) in hard times, because they can buy it for less money than pure wheat. I do not believe there is a family among the common people of Syria which has not suffered at one time or another from "tare-sickness." Having tasted the gall of this affliction a few times myself, I do not at all wonder at the Syrians' belief that tares must have come into the world by the Devil. And what I still remember with both amusement and sympathy are the heartfelt, withering imprecations which the afflicted ones always showered upon the seller of the "tarey wheat." When the food had taken real effect and the staggering, nauseated members of a family felt compelled to allow nature to take its course, the gasps and groans punctuated the ejaculations, "May God destroy his home!" "May the gold turn into dust in his hands!" "May he spend the price of what he sold us at the funerals of his children!"—and so forth.

Do you feel now the force of the allusion to the tares in the parable? "So the servants of the householder came and said unto him, Sir, didst not thou sow good seed in thy field? from whence then hath it tares? He said unto them, An enemy hath done this."

Enemies are of course always disposed to injure one another, and in an agricultural country like Syria harm is often done to property for revenge. So the scattering of tares for this purpose in a newly sown wheat-field is not utterly unnatural or unthinkable. But the reference in the parable is to a belief which is prevalent in some districts in Syria, to the effect that in spite of all that the sower can do to prevent it, the tares do appear mysteriously in fields where only wheat had been sown. Some evil power introduces the noxious plant. Once I listened to a heated controversy on the subject between some Syrian landowners and an American missionary. The landowners clung to the belief that tares would appear in a field even if no tare seed was ever planted in that field, while the son of the West insisted that no such growth could take place without the seed having first been introduced into the field in some natural way. The fight was a draw.

"The servants said unto him, Wilt thou then that we go and gather them up? But he said, Nay, lest while ye gather up the tares, ye root up also the wheat with them."

The attempt is often made to pull up the hated tares from among the wheat, but in vain. The concluding admonition in the parable may well be taken to heart by every hasty reformer of the type of a certain regenerator of society, who, when asked to proceed slowly, said, "The fact is I am in a hurry, and God is not!"

In the same chapter (Matt. XIII) occurs the parable of the "leaven." "The kingdom of heaven is like unto leaven, which a woman took, and hid in three measures of meal, till the whole was leavened." The setting of this short parable in Syrian life is given in another chapter. But I mention it here in order to give my comment on a rather strange interpretation of the parable which came recently to my knowledge. In the course of a conversation I had with a prominent Baptist minister not long since, he stated to me that certain interpreters assert that the leaven in this parable meant the corruption which has come into the Christian Church, etc. My friend was anxious to know whether to my knowledge the Syrians associated leaven with corruption.

This interpretation echoes an ancient idea of leaven of which modern Syrians have no knowledge. They hold the leaven in high and reverential esteem. To them it is the symbol of growth and fecundity. In many of the rural districts of Syria, upon approaching the door of her future home the bride is given the *khamera* (the lump of leaven) which she pastes on the upper door-sill and passes under it into the house. As she performs the solemn act her friends exclaim, "May you be as blessed and as fruitful as the *khamera*!"

However, it is a well-known fact to readers of ancient records that in the earliest times bread was entirely unleavened. When the Israelites were roaming tribes they ate and offered to Jehovah unleavened bread. The Arab tribes of to-day on the borders of Syria eat no leavened bread. They believe that it tends to reduce the vitality and endurance of the body. Perhaps the real reason for preferring the unleavened bread is that it is much easier to make, and dispenses with taking care of the lump of leaven between bakings, which is not so convenient for roaming tribes to do. The use of unleavened bread for so many generations among the Israelites constituted its sacredness, and it was the conservatism of religion which still called for unleavened bread for the offering, even after leavened bread had become universally the daily food of the people.

So to the ancients the fermentation in the process of leavening was considered corruption. It was something which entered into the lump and soured it. The New Testament use of the word "leaven" as meaning corruption is purely figurative, and signifies influence, or bad doctrine. It was in this sense that Jesus used the word when he said to his disciples: [3] "Take heed and beware of the leaven of the Pharisees and of the Sadducees"; and again: [4] "Take heed, beware of the leaven of the Pharisees, and of the leaven of Herod." The fact that the disciples did not understand at first what the Master meant shows that to the general public "leaven" and "corruption" were not synonymous terms. Had they been, it is certain that Jesus never would have said, "The kingdom of heaven is like unto leaven."

The fifteenth chapter of St. Luke's Gospel contains the parables of the lost sheep, the lost coin, and the prodigal son. The parable of the lost sheep is discussed in another chapter. The parable of the lost coin portrays a very familiar scene in the ordinary Syrian home. "What woman," says the Master, "having ten pieces of silver, if she lose one piece, doth not light a candle, and sweep the house, and seek diligently till she find it? And when she hath found it, she calleth her friends and her neighbors together, saying, Rejoice with me; for I have found the piece which I had lost."

The candle spoken of here is a little olive-oil lamp—an earthen saucer, with a protruding lip curled up at one point in the rim for the wick. How often have I held that flickering light for my mother while she searched for a lost coin or some other precious object. The common Syrian house has one door and one or two small windows, with wooden shutters, without glass. [5] Consequently the interior of the house is dimly lighted, especially in the winter season. The scarcity of money in the hands of the people makes the loss of a coin, of the value of that which is mentioned in the parable (about sixteen cents), a sad event. The little house is searched with eager thoroughness—"diligently." The straw mats, cushions, and sheepskins which cover the floor are turned over, and the earthen floor swept. The search continues, with diligence and prayerful expectations, until the lost coin is found. The Arabic Bible states that the gladdened woman "calls her *women* neighbors and friends (*jaratiha wesedikatiha*), saying, Rejoice with me; for I have found the piece which I had lost." The singling out of the *women* neighbors is significant here. As a rule the loss of a precious coin by a woman calls her husband's wrath upon her, regardless of whether the coin had been earned by her or by him. The *women friends* have a keen fellow-feeling in such matters. They keep one another's secrets from the men, and rejoice when one of their number escapes an unpleasant situation.

The total meaning of this parable is plain as it is most precious. Through this common occurrence in a Syrian home, Jesus impresses upon the minds of his hearers, as well as upon the consciousness of all mankind, the infinite worth of the human soul, and the Father's love and care for it. "Likewise, I say unto you, there is joy in the presence of the angels of God over one sinner that repenteth."

The parable of the prodigal son follows immediately that of the lost coin. "A certain man had two sons: and the younger of them said to his father, Father, give me the portion of goods that falleth to me. And he divided unto them his living." The first thing in this parable to challenge the attention is the father's quick compliance with the request of his son. "And he divided unto them his living." The custom of a father dividing his property among his grown sons before his death prevails much more extensively in the East than in the West. As a rule neither the law nor custom gives legal standing to a will. Sometimes the father's wishes with regard to how his property should be divided after his death are carried out by his sons. But as a general rule the father who does not divide his property legally between his sons before his death leaves to them a situation fraught with danger. Litigation in such cases is very slow and uncertain.

It was such a situation, no doubt, which led the man referred to in the twelfth chapter of Luke, the thirteenth verse, to say to Jesus, "Master, speak to my brother, that he divide the inheritance with me. And he said unto him, Man, who made me a judge or a divider over you?" And we may easily infer what Jesus thought of that particular case from his saying which follows immediately his answer to this man. "And he said unto them, Take heed, and beware of covetousness: for a man's life consisteth not in the abundance of the things which he possesseth." So the father of the prodigal son acted normally when he divided his substance between his two sons.

"And not many days after the younger son gathered all together, and took his journey into a far country, and there wasted his substance with riotous living." The singling out of the younger son for this adventure comports with a highly cherished Oriental tradition. The elder son, who was the first-born male child in this household, could not very well be made to commit such an act. In a Syrian family the *bikkr* (the first-born son) stands next to the father in the esteem, not only of the members of his own household, but of the community at large. He cannot be supposed to be so rash, so unmindful of his birthright, as to break the sacred family circle, and to waste his inheritance in riotous living.

"And when he had spent all, there arose a mighty famine in that land; and he began to be in want. And he went and joined himself to a citizen of that country; and he sent him into his fields to feed swine. And he would fain have been filled with the husks that the swine did eat; and no man gave unto him."

To be a swineherd, or a "swine-shepherd," is the most contemptible occupation an Oriental can think of. It is no wonder at all to me that the Gospel writers make the destination of the "legion" of devils which Jesus cast out of the man "in the country of the Gadarenes," a herd of swine. [6] You cannot hire a Syrian to make a pet of a "little piggie." If he did, he would be called "*Abu khenzier*" (pig man) for the rest of his life, and transmit the unenviable title to his posterity, "even unto the third and fourth generation."

The word "husks" in the English version is not a correct rendering of the original term. The marginal note in the Revised Version reads, "the pods of the carob tree." The Arabic version says simply *kherrûb* (carob). The carob tree is very common in the lowlands of Syria. It is a large tree of dense foliage, and round, glossy, dark-green leaves. The pods it bears measure from five to ten inches in length, are flat, and largely horn-shaped. I do not know why the English translators of the Bible called those pods "husks." They are sold in almost every town in western Syria for food. Children are very fond of *kherrûb*. Some of the pods contain no small amount of sugar. In my boyhood days, a pocketful of *kherrûb*, which I procured for a penny, was to me rather a treat. The older people, however, do not esteem *kherrûb* so highly as do the children. The bulk of it is so out of proportion to the sugar it contains that its poverty is proverbial in the land. Of one whose conversation is luxuriant in words and barren of ideas it is said, "It is like eating *kherrûb*; you have to consume a cord of wood in order to get an ounce of sweet." By eating these pods, the poor people seem to themselves "to have been filled" while in reality they have received but little nutrition. Therefore *kherrûb* is generally eaten by animals.

It may be observed that the saying in the parable, "and he would fain have been filled with *kherrûb* that the swine did eat: and no man gave unto him," simply describes the prodigal's poverty. For as a "swine-shepherd" the "*kherrûb* that the swine did eat" was certainly very accessible to him. The purpose of the passage is to draw the contrast between the rich parental home which the prodigal had willingly left and the extremely humble fare on which in his wretched state he was compelled to subsist.

The return of the prodigal son to his father's house, impoverished but penitent, the affectionate magnanimity of the father toward his son, and the spreading of the feast in honor of the occasion, are acts of humility and generosity which cannot be said to be exclusively Oriental. But the command of the father to his servants, "Bring hither the fatted calf and kill it; and let us eat and be merry," brings out the idea of the *zebihat* (animal sacrifice) with which the West is not familiar.

The ancient custom, whose echoes have not yet died out in the East, was that the host honored his guest most highly by killing a sheep at the threshold of the house, upon the guest's arrival, and inviting him to step over the blood into the house. This act formed the "blood covenant" between the guest and his host. It made them one. To us one of the most cordial and dignified expressions in inviting a guest, especially from a distant town, was, "If God ever favors us with a visit from you, we will kill a *zebihat!*"

In his great rejoicing in the return of his son, the father of the prodigal is made to receive him as he would a most highly honored guest. "The fatted calf"—and not only a sheep—is killed as the *zebihat* of a new covenant between a loving father and his son, who "was dead and is alive again; was lost, and is found." [7]

The parable of the "treasure hid in a field" [8] alludes to a very interesting phase of Syrian thought. "Again, the kingdom of heaven is like unto a treasure hid in a field, the which when a man hath found, he hideth, and for joy thereof goeth and selleth all that he hath, and buyeth that field."

I cannot refrain from quoting again in this connection the famous commentator, Adam Clarke. Speaking of this parable, he says: "We are not to imagine that the *treasure* here mentioned, and to which the gospel salvation is likened, means a *pot or chest* of money hidden in the field, but rather a gold or silver *mine*, which he who found out could not get at, or work, without turning up the field, and for this purpose he bought it. Mr. Wakefield's observation is very just: 'There is no sense in the *purchase* of a field for a *pot* of money, which he might have carried away very *readily* and as *honestly*, too, as by overreaching the owner by an unjust purchase.' ... From this view of the subject, the translation of this verse, given above, will appear proper—a *hidden treasure*, when applied to a *rich mine*, is more proper than a *treasure hid*, which applies better to a *pot of money* deposited there, which I suppose was our translator's opinion; and *kept secret*, or *concealed*, will apply better to the subject of his discovery till he made the purchase, than *hideth*, for which there could be no occasion, when the pot was already *hidden*, and the place known only to himself."

I have inserted here this double quotation, italics and all, in order to show how when the real facts are not known to a writer the temptation to play on words becomes irresistible. In this exposition the simple parable is treated as a legal document. Every word of it is subjected to careful scrutiny. "Hid" is converted into "hidden," and "concealed" is summoned to supplant "hideth," in order to make the "treasure" mean a vast deposit of gold ore, and get the poor Syrian peasant into the mining business.

The facts in the case, however, stand opposed to this explanation. I am absolutely safe in saying that every man, woman, and child in Syria understands that this parable refers simply and purely to a treasure of gold and silver which had been buried in a field by human hands. The entanglement of the commentator just quoted in the literary fault of the parable is inexcusable.

The New Testament writer might have said, not that the man in the parable *found* the treasure, but that he was *led* by certain signs *to believe* that a treasure lay hidden in the field. However, this is not the Oriental way of stating things, nor should the speaker in parables be denied the freedom of the poet and the artist to manipulate the particulars in such a way as to make them serve the central purpose of his production.

I could fill a book with the stories of hidden treasures which charmed my boyhood days in Syria. I have already put into print [9] a detailed account of my personal experience in digging for a hidden treasure, which will clearly show that the securing of such riches is not always so easy to diggers as the quotation just cited would make one believe. In order to show the attitude of Syrians in general toward this subject, I will quote the following from my own personal account:—

"In Syria it is universally believed that hidden treasures may be found anywhere in the land, and especially among ancient ruins. This belief rests on the simple truth that the tribes and clans of Syria, having from time immemorial lived in a state of warfare, have hidden their treasures in the ground, especially on the eve of battles.

"Furthermore, the wars of the past being wars of extermination, the vanquished could not return to reclaim their hidden wealth; therefore the ground is the keeper of vast riches. The tales of the digging and finding of such treasures fill the country. There are thrilling tales of treasures in various localities. Gold and other valuables are said to have been dug up in sealed earthen jars, often by the merest accident, in the ground, in the walls of houses, under enchanted trees, and in sepulchers. From earliest childhood the people's minds are fed on these tales, and they grow up with all their senses alert to the remotest suggestions of such possibilities."

The writer of the parable did not need to explain the situation to his Oriental readers. The mere mention of a "hidden treasure" was sufficient to make them know what the words meant. His supreme purpose was to impress them with the matchless worth of the kingdom of heaven which Christ came to reveal to the world.

[1] Revised Version.
[2] Matt. xiii: 34.
[3] Matt. xvi: 6.
[4] Mark viii: 15.
[5] See the author's autobiography, *A Far Journey*, chap. 1, entitled "My Father's House."
[6] Matt. viii: 32; Mark v: 13; Luke viii: 33.

[7] For the reason why the mother of the prodigal is not mentioned in the parable, see pages 207 and 334.
[8] Matt. xiii: 44.
[9] *Atlantic Monthly*, December, 1915. This story, with other essays, will soon appear in book form.

Chapter Seven – Swearing

Perhaps the one phase of his speech which lays the Oriental open to the charge of unveracity is his much swearing. Of course this evil habit knows no geographical boundaries and no racial limits. However, probably because of their tendency to be profuse, intense, and positive in speech, the Orientals no doubt have more than their legitimate share of swearing. But it should be kept in mind that in that part of the world swearing is not looked upon with the same disapproval and contempt as in America; swearing by the name of the Deity has always been considered the most sacred and solemn affirmation of a statement. It is simply calling God to witness that what has been said is the sacred truth. Thus in the twenty-first chapter of the book of Genesis Abimelech asks Abraham, "Now therefore swear unto me here by God that thou wilt not deal falsely with me, nor with my son, nor with my son's son." "And Abraham said, I will swear."

St. Paul employs this type of speech in a milder form, after the New Testament fashion, in the opening verse of the twelfth chapter of his Epistle to the Romans, where he says: "I beseech you, therefore, brethren, *by the mercies of God*, that ye present your bodies a living sacrifice, holy, acceptable unto God, which is your reasonable service." In the opening verse of the ninth chapter of the Epistle to the Romans, Paul succeeds in an elegant manner in dispensing with swearing altogether, when he says: "I say the truth in Christ, I lie not, my conscience also bearing me witness in the Holy Ghost."

Generally speaking, however, the custom of swearing after the manner of the Old Testament has undergone no change in Syria since the days of Abraham. Swearing is an integral element in Oriental speech. Instinctively the speaker turns his eyes and lifts his hands toward heaven and says, "By Allah, what I have said is right and true. *Yeshhedo-Allah* [God witnesseth] to the truth of my words." In a similar manner, and as in a score of places in the Old Testament, the maker of a statement is asked by his hearer to swear by God as a solemn assurance that his statement is true and sincere.

The Mohammedan law, which is the law of modern Syria, demands swearing in judicial contests. The judge awards the accuser—that is, the plaintiff—the right to lead the defendant to any shrine he may choose, and cause him to swear the *yemîn* (solemn oath) as a final witness to his innocence. By this act the plaintiff places his adversary in the hands of the Supreme Judge, whose judgments are "true and righteous altogether." A false oath is supposed to bring awful retribution upon its maker and upon his posterity.

Of such importance is this mode of speech to Orientals that the Israelites thought of Jehovah Himself as making such affirmations. In the twenty-second chapter of Genesis we have the words, "By myself have I sworn, saith the Lord." Further light is thrown on this point by the explanation given to the verse just quoted in the sixth chapter of the Epistle to the Hebrews, where it is said, "For when God made promise to Abraham, because he could swear by no greater, he swore by himself."

I have no doubt that this thought of God swearing by himself sprang from the custom of Oriental aristocrats of sealing a vow, or solemnly affirming a statement, or an intention to do some daring deed, by saying, "I swear by my head"—an oath which, whenever I heard it in my youth, filled me with awe. Thus, also, in the sixty-second chapter of Isaiah we have the words, "The Lord hath sworn by his right hand, and by the arm of his strength."

Among the Mohammedans, swearing "by the most high God" and "by the life of the Prophet" and "by the exalted Koran" in affirmation of almost every statement, is universal. The Christians swear by God, Christ, the Virgin, the Cross, the Saints, the repose of their dead, the Holy City, the Eucharist, Heaven, great holidays, and many other names. A father swears by the life of a dear child, and sons of distinguished fathers swear by them. "By the life of my father, I am telling the truth," is a very common expression. The antiquity of this custom is made evident by the passage in the thirty-first chapter of Genesis and the fifty-third verse: "And Jacob sware by the fear of his father Isaac." However, the word "fear" does violence to the real meaning of the verse, which the Arabic version rescues by saying, "And Jacob swore by the *heybet* [benignity, or beautiful dignity] of his father." He swore by that which he and others loved, and not feared, in his father.

But what must seem to Americans utterly ridiculous is the Oriental habit of swearing by the mustache and the beard, which is, however, one phase of swearing by the head. To swear by one's mustache, or beard, means to pledge the integrity of one's manhood. "I swear by this," is said solemnly by a man with his hand upon his mustache. Swearing by the beard is supposed to carry more weight because, as a rule, it is worn by the older men. To speak disrespectfully of one's mustache or beard, or to curse the beard of a person's father, is to invite serious trouble.

The sacredness of the beard to Orientals goes back to the remote past when all the hair of the head and the face was considered sacred. Growing a beard is still esteemed a solemn act in Syria, so much so that, having let his beard grow, one cannot shave it off without becoming a by-word in the community. To speak of the scissors or of a razor in the presence of one wearing a beard, especially if he be a priest, or of the aristocracy, is considered a deep insult to him. Such unseemly conduct seldom fails to precipitate a fight. In 2 Samuel, the tenth chapter, fourth verse, we have the record of Hanun's disgraceful treatment of David's men, whom he had thought to be spies. "Wherefore Hanun took David's servants, and shaved off the one half of their beards, and cut off their garments in the middle, even to their buttocks, and sent them away. When they told it unto David, he sent to meet them, because the men *were greatly ashamed*: and the king said, Tarry at Jericho *until your beards be grown*, and then return."

It is because of this ancient conception of the hair that the Syrians still swear by the mustache and the beard, although the majority of them know not the real reason why they do so.

I remember distinctly how proud I was in my youth to put my hand upon my mustache, when it was yet not even large enough to be respectfully noticed, and swear by it *as a man*. I recall also to what roars of laughter I would provoke my elders at such times, to my great dismay.

Here it may easily be seen that swearing in the Orient had so lost its original sacredness and become so vulgar, even as far back as the time of Christ, that He deemed it necessary to give the unqualified command, "Swear not at all: neither by heaven, for it is God's throne, nor by the earth, for it is his footstool: neither by Jerusalem, for it is the city of the great King. Neither shalt thou swear by thy head, because thou canst not make one hair white or black. But let your communication be yea, yea; nay, nay; for whatsoever is more than these cometh of evil." This was perhaps the most difficult command to obey that Jesus ever gave to his countrymen.

Chapter Eight - Four Characteristics

Of the other characteristics of Oriental speech, I wish to speak of four before I bring this part of my book to a close.

The first, the many and picturesque dialects. The entire absence of the public school, the scarcity of other educational institutions, as well as of books and periodicals, and the extreme slowness of transportation, have always tended to perpetuate the multitude of dialects in the speech of the Syrian people. The common language of the land is the Arabic, which is divided into two types—the classical and the common, or the language of learning and that of daily speech. The classical language is one, but the common language is a labyrinth of dialects. Each section of that small country has

60

its *lehjah* (accent), and it is no exaggeration to say that each town within those sections has a *lehjah* of its own. Certain letters of the alphabet are also sounded differently in different localities. Thus, for an example, the word for "stood" is pronounced *qam* in certain localities, and *aam* in others. The word for "male" is pronounced *zeker* by some communities, and *deker* by others.

That such a state of things prevailed also in ancient Israel and in New Testament times is very evident. In the twelfth chapter of the Book of Judges we have the record of a fight between the Gileadites and the Ephraimites, in which we find the following statement: "And the Gileadites took the passages of Jordan before the Ephraimites: and it was so, that when those Ephraimites which were escaped said, Let me go over; that the men of Gilead said unto him, Art thou an Ephraimite? If he said, Nay; then said they unto him, Say now Shibboleth: and he said Sibboleth: *for he could not frame to pronounce it right*. Then they took him, and slew him."

This simple means of identification might be used in present-day Syria with equal success.

In the fourteenth chapter of St. Mark's Gospel we have another striking illustration of this characteristic of Oriental speech, in Peter's experience in the palace of the high priest. In the fifty-third verse it is said: "And they led Jesus away to the high priest: and with him were assembled all the chief priests and the elders and the scribes. And Peter followed him afar off, even into the palace of the high priest." The record continues (verses 66-71): "And as Peter was beneath in the palace, there cometh one of the maids of the high priest: and when she saw Peter warming himself, she looked upon him, and said, And thou also wast with Jesus of Nazareth. But he denied, saying, I know not, neither understand I what thou sayest. And he went out into the porch.... And a little after, they that stood by said again to Peter, Surely thou art one of them: for thou art a Galilaean, *and thy speech agreeth thereto*. [1] But he began to curse and to swear, saying, I know not this man of whom ye speak."

Poor Peter! the more he swore and cursed the more clearly he revealed his identity. His cowardice might have concealed him, but for his dialect. He spoke the dialect of Galilee in the city of Jerusalem, and so far as the identification of his person was concerned, even a certificate from the authorities of the town of his birth, testifying to his being a native of Galilee, could not have so effectively served that purpose.

The second characteristic is the juvenile habit of imploring "in season and out of season" when asking a favor. To try to exert "undue" influence, virtually to beg in most persuasive tones, is an Oriental habit which to an American must seem unendurable. Of the many illustrations of this custom which fill my memory I will relate the following incident, which I once heard a man relate to my father.

This man had bought, for six hundred piasters, a piece of land which had been given as a *nezer* (vow) to our Greek Orthodox Church. After he had given his note for the sum and secured the deed, it occurred to him that the price was too high, and, being himself a son of the Church, that he ought to secure the land for four hundred piasters. So, as he stated, he went to Beyrout, the seat of our bishop, where he stayed three days. By constant petitioning, he secured the privilege of interviewing the bishop four times on the subject. With great glee he stated that at the last interview he refused to rise from his seat at the feet of that long-suffering ecclesiastic until his petition was granted.

One of the most striking examples of this characteristic is the parable of the unrighteous judge, in the eighteenth chapter of Luke. "There was in a city a judge, which feared not God, neither regarded man: and there was a widow in that city, and she came unto him saying, Avenge me [the original is "do me justice"] of mine adversary. And he would not for a while: but afterward he said within himself, Though I fear not God, nor regard man, yet because this widow troubleth me, I will avenge her, *lest by her continual coming she weary me.*"

Here is a case—by no means a rare exception in that country—where a judge rendered a verdict against his own best judgment in sheer self-defense. And I must say that, knowing such Oriental tendencies as I do, especially as manifested by widows, I am in deep sympathy with the judge.

Yet it was this very persistence in petitioning the Father of all men which gave mankind the lofty psalms and tender prayers of our Scriptures. It was this persistent filial pleading and imploring which made Israel turn again and again to the "God of righteousness" and say, "We have sinned," and ask for a deeper revealing of his ways to them. Job's cry, "Though he slay me, yet will I trust in him," may not be the proper language of modern etiquette, but it certainly is the language of religion. In the very parable just quoted, Jesus recommends to his disciples the insistence of the widow as a means to draw the benediction of heaven upon them, and to secure for them justification at the hands of the righteous judge. Honest seekers after spiritual gifts should not be averse to imitating this Oriental trait. They should never be afraid to come to their Father again and again for his gracious blessing, or refrain from "storming the gates of heaven with prayer."

The third characteristic of Oriental speech is its intimacy and unreserve. Mere implications which are so common to reserved and guarded speech leave a void in the Oriental heart. It is because of this that the Orientals have always craved "signs and wonders," and interpreted natural phenomena in terms of direct miraculous communications from God to convince them that He cared for them. Although Gideon was speaking with Jehovah Himself, who promised to help him to save his kinsmen from the Midianites, he asked for a more tangible, more definite sign. We are told in the sixth chapter of Judges, thirty-sixth verse: "And Gideon said unto God, If thou wilt save Israel by mine hand, as thou hast spoken, behold, I will put a fleece of wool on the threshing-floor; if there be dew on the fleece only, and it be dry upon all the ground, then shall I know that thou wilt save Israel by mine hand, as thou hast spoken. And it was so." But Gideon, still unsatisfied, speaks again in childlike simplicity and intimacy; "Let not thine anger be kindled against me, and I will speak but this once: let me make trial, I pray thee, but this once with the fleece; let it now be dry only upon the fleece, and upon all the ground let there be dew. And God did so that night."

It is not at all uncommon for old and tried friends in Syria to give and ask for affectionate assurances, that they do love one another. Such expressions are the wine of life. Especially when new confidences are exchanged or great favors asked, a man turns with guileless eyes to his trusted friend and says, "Now you love me; I say you love me, don't you?" "My soul, my eyes," answers the other, "you know what is in my heart toward you; you know and the Creator knows!" Then the request is made. One of the noblest and tenderest passages in the New Testament, a passage whose spirit has fed the strength of the Christian missionaries throughout the ages, is that portion of the twenty-first chapter of St. John's Gospel where Jesus speaks to Peter in this intimate Syrian fashion. How sweet and natural it sounds to a son of the East! "So when they had dined, Jesus saith to Simon Peter, Simon, son of Jonas, lovest thou me?" How characteristic also is Peter's answer, "Yea, Lord; thou knowest that I love thee." Then came the precious request, "Feed my lambs." Three times did the affectionate Master knock at the door of Peter's heart, till the poor impetuous disciple cried, "Lord, thou knowest all things; thou knowest that I love thee. Jesus saith unto him, Feed my sheep."

The fourth characteristic of Oriental speech is its unqualified positiveness. Outside the small circles of Europeanized Syrians, such qualifying phrases as "in my opinion," "so it seems to me," "as I see it," and the like, are almost entirely absent from Oriental speech. The Oriental is never so cautious in his speech as a certain American editor of a religious paper, who in speaking of Cain described him as "the *alleged* murderer of Abel"! Such expressions, also, are rarely used in the Bible, and then only in the New Testament, in which Greek influence plays no small part. Thus in the seventh chapter of his second Epistle to the Corinthians, Paul, in giving his opinion on marriage said, "*I suppose*, therefore, that this is good for the present distress," and so forth. I am not aware that this form of speech is used anywhere in the entire Old Testament.

The language of the Oriental is that of sentiment and conviction, and not of highly differentiated and specialized thought. When you say to him, "I think this object is beautiful," if he does not think it is so, he says, "No, it is not beautiful." Although he is expressing his own individual opinion, he does not take the trouble to make that perfectly clear: if an object is not beautiful to him, it *is not* beautiful.

From an intellectual and social standpoint, this mode of speech may be considered a serious defect. So do children express themselves. But it should be kept in mind that the Oriental mind is that of the prophet and the seer, and not of the scientist and the philosopher. It is the mind which has proven the most suitable transmissive agency of divine revelation.

When the seer beholds a vision of the things that are eternal, he cannot speak of it as a supposition or a guess, or transmit it with intellectual caution and timidity. "Thus saith the Lord." "The word of the Lord came unto me saying, Son of man, prophesy." When we speak of the deepest realities of life, we do not beset our utterances with qualifying phrases. True love, deep sorrow, a real vision of spiritual things transcend all speculative speech; they press with irresistible might for direct and authoritative expression.

Take for an example Jesus' matchless declaration: "The Spirit of the Lord is upon me, because he hath anointed me to preach the gospel [glad tidings] to the poor; he hath sent me to heal the broken-hearted, to preach deliverance to the captives, and recovering of sight to the blind, to set at liberty them that are bruised, to preach the acceptable year of the Lord." [2] How would this great utterance sound if given in the nice, cautious language of an "up-to-date" thinker? What force would it carry if put in this form, "It seems to me, although I may be entirely mistaken, that something like what may be termed the 'Spirit of the Lord' is upon me, and I feel that, in my own limited way, I must preach the Gospel"?

Of course reckless, dogmatic assertions from the pulpit are never wise nor profitable. Ultimately, whether in the realms of science or spiritual experience, the facts are the things which will count. Nevertheless, it must be admitted that the modern pulpit suffers to a large extent from overcautiousness. By many ministers the facts are evaluated more in an intellectual than in a spiritual sense. Hence that cautiousness in utterance which is seriously threatening the spirit of prophecy and the authority of real spiritual *experience* in the religious teachers of the present day. Legitimate intellectual caution should never be allowed to degenerate into spiritual timidity, nor the knowledge of outward things to put out the prophetic fire in the soul. There is, no doubt, much food for thought in the following legend. It is said of a preacher, who was apparently determined not to make "rash statements," that in speaking to his people on repentance he had this for his final word: "If you do not repent, as it were, and be converted, in a measure, you will be damned, to a certain extent." The congregation that has such a preacher is damned already! And I perceive some difference between such a preacher and Him who says, "Verily, I say unto you, except ye be converted, and become as little children, ye shall not enter into the kingdom of heaven." [3]

This seeming weakness in Oriental speech and in the Bible is in reality tremendous spiritual strength. Through our sacred Scriptures we hear the voices of those great Oriental prophets who spoke as they saw and felt; as seers, and not as logicians. And it was indeed most fortunate for the world that the Bible was written in an age of instinctive listening to the divine Voice, and in a country whose juvenile modes of speech protected the "rugged maxims" of the Scriptures from the weakening influences of an overstrained intellectualism.

[1] See also Matt. xxvi: 73.　　[2] Luke iv: 18.　　[3] Matt. xviii: 3.

Part Three - Bread and Salt

Chapter One - The Sacred 'Aish

To an Oriental the phrase "bread and salt" is of sacred import. The saying, "There is bread and salt between us," which has been prevalent in the East from time immemorial, is equal to saying, "We are bound together by a solemn covenant." To say of one that he "knows not the significance of bread and salt" is to stigmatize him as a base ingrate.

A noble foe refuses to "taste the salt" of his adversary—that is, to eat with him—so long as he feels disinclined to be reconciled to him. Such a foe dreads the thought of repudiating the covenant which the breaking of bread together forms. In the rural districts of Syria, much more than in the cities, is still observed the ancient custom that a man on an important mission should not eat his host's bread until the errand is made known. The covenant of "bread and salt" should not be entered into before the attitude of the host toward his guest's mission is fully known. If the request is granted, then the meal is enjoyed as a fraternal affirmation of the agreement just made. So in the twenty-fourth chapter of the Book of Genesis we are told that Abraham's servant, who had gone to Mesopotamia, "unto the city of Nahor," to bring a wife of his master's kindred to his son Isaac, refused to eat at Laban's table before he had told his errand. With characteristic Oriental hospitality the brother of Rebekah, after hearing his sister's story, sought Abraham's faithful servant, "and, behold, he stood by the camels at the well. And he said, Come in, thou blessed of the Lord; wherefore standest thou without? for I have prepared the house, and room for the camels. And the man came into the house...And there was set meat before him to eat: but he said, *I will not eat, until I have told mine errand.*" [1] The errand having been told, "the servant brought forth jewels of silver, and jewels of gold, and raiment, and gave them to Rebekah...*And they did eat and drink*, he and the men that were with him." [2]

Of all his enemies, the writer of the forty-first Psalm considered the "familiar friend" who went back on his simple covenant to be the worst. "Yea," he cries, mournfully, "mine own familiar friend, in whom I trusted, which did eat my bread, hath lifted up his heel against me."

As the son of a Syrian family I was brought up to think of bread as possessing a mystic sacred significance. I never would step on a piece of bread fallen in the road, but would pick it up, press it to my lips for reverence, and place it in a wall or some other place where it would not be trodden upon.

What always seemed to me to be one of the noblest traditions of my people was their reverence for the 'aish (bread; literally, "the life-giver"). While breaking bread together we would not rise to salute an arriving guest, whatever his social rank. Whether spoken or not, our excuse for not rising and engaging in the cordial Oriental salutation before the meal was ended, was our reverence for the food (*hirmetel-'aish*). We could, however, and always did, invite the newcomer most urgently to partake of the repast.

At least once each year, for many years, I carried the *korban* (the bread offering) to the *mizbeh* (altar of sacrifice) in our village church, as an offering for the repose of the souls of our dead as well as for our own spiritual security. Bread was one of the elements of the holy Eucharist. The mass always closed with the handing by the priest to the members of the congregation of small pieces of consecrated bread. The Gospel taught us also that Christ was the "bread of life."

The *'aish* was something more than mere matter. Inasmuch as it sustained life, it was God's own life made tangible for his child, man, to feed upon. The Most High himself fed our hunger. Does not the Psalmist say, "Thou openest thine hand, and satisfieth the desire of every living thing"? Where else could our daily bread come from?

[1] Verses 30-33.
[2] Verses 53-54. The word "drink," which is frequently used in the Bible in connection with the word "eat," does not necessarily refer to wine drinking. The expression "food and drink" is current in Syria, and means simply "board." An employer says to an employee, "I will pay you so much wages, and your food and drink" (aklek washirbek). The drink may be nothing but water.

Chapter Two - "Our Daily Bread"

I have often heard it said by "up-to-date" religionists in this country that the saying in the Lord's Prayer, "Give us this day our daily bread," was at best a beggar's lazy petition. It has been suggested that those words should be omitted from the prayer, because they pertain to "material things." And at any rate we can get our daily bread only by working for it.

Yes; and the Oriental understands all that. But he perceives also that by working for his daily bread he does not *create* it, but simply *finds* it. The prayer, "Give us this day our daily bread" is a note of pure gratitude to the "Giver of all good and perfect gifts." The Oriental does not know "material things" as the Occidental knows them. To him organic chemistry does not take the place of God. He is, in his totality, God-centered. His center of gravity is the altar and not the factory, and back of his prayer for daily bread is the momentum of ages of mystic contemplation. The Oriental finds kinship, not with those who go for their daily bread no farther than the bakery, but with the writer of this modern psalm:—

"Back of the loaf is the snowy flour,
    Back of the flour the mill;
    Back of the mill is the wheat and the shower
    And the sun and the Father's will."

It is not my purpose to exaggerate the piety and moral rectitude of the Oriental. I am fully aware of the fact that he is lamentably lacking in his efforts to rise to the height of his noblest traditions. Nevertheless, those who know the Oriental's inner life know also that from seed-time until harvest, and until the bread is placed upon the family board, this man's attitude toward the "staff of life" is essentially religious. In the name of God he casts the seed into the soil; in the name of God he thrusts the sickle into the ripe harvest; in the name of God he scatters his sheaves on the threshing floor and grinds his grain at the mill; and in the name of God his wife kneads the dough, bakes the bread, and serves it to her family.

In my childhood days "kneading-day" at our house was always of peculiar significance to me. I had no toys or story-books to engage my attention, and it was with the greatest interest that I watched my mother go through the process of kneading. Her pious words and actions made kneading a sort of religious service.

After making the sign of the cross and invoking the Holy Name, she drew the required quantity of flour out of a small opening near the bottom of the earthen barrel in which the precious meal was stored. It was out of such a barrel that the widow of "Zarephath which belongeth to Zidon" drew the "handful of meal" she had, and made of it a cake for Elijah, for which favor the fiery prophet prayed that the widow's barrel of meal "shall not waste."

Then my mother packed the flour in the shape of a crescent on one side of the large earthen *maajan* (kneading basin) which is about thirty inches in diameter. She dissolved the salt in warm water, which she poured in the basin by the embankment of flour. Then with a "God bless" she took out the leaven—a lump of dough saved from the former baking—which she had buried in flour to keep it "from corruption," that is, from overfermentation. This leaven she dissolved carefully in the salt water, and by slowly mixing the meal with this fluid, she "hid" the leaven in the meal. It was this process which Jesus mentioned very briefly in the parable of the leaven in the thirteenth chapter of St. Matthew's Gospel. "The kingdom of heaven is like unto leaven, which a woman took and hid in three measures of meal, till the whole was leavened."

The kneading done, my mother smoothed the surface of the blessed lump, dipped her hand in water, and with the edge of her palm marked a deep cross the whole length of the diameter of the basin, crossed herself three times, while she muttered an invocation, and then covered the basin and left the dough to rise. The same pious attitude was resumed when the raised dough was made into small loaves, during the baking, and whenever the mother of the family put her hand into the basin where the loaves were kept, to take out bread for her family's needs.

Does it now seem strange, unnatural, or in any way out of harmony with the trend of her whole life, for such a woman to pray, "Give us this day our daily bread"? Shall we receive the gifts and forget the Giver? However circuitous our way to our daily bread may be, the fact remains that we do feed on God's own life. "The earth is the Lord's and the fullness thereof."

The use of iron stoves was unknown to the Syrians in my childhood days; and this modern convenience is now used only by some of the well-to-do people in the large cities. The rank and file of the people, as in the days of ancient Israel, still bake their bread at semi-public ovens, a few of which are found in every village and town. This baking-place is mentioned often in the Bible, but the word "oven" in the English translation is somewhat misleading. It is so because the *tennûr* (translated "oven" in the Bible) is unknown to the English-speaking world, if not to the entire Occident. The *tennûr* is a huge earthen tube about three feet in diameter and about five feet long; it is sunk in the ground within a small, roughly constructed hut. The women bake their bread at the *tennûr* in turn, certain days being assigned to certain families. The one baking comprises from one hundred to two hundred loaves. The fuel, which consists of small branches of trees, and of thistles and straw, is thrown into the *tennûr* in large quantities. It is to this that Jesus alludes in the passage, "If then God so clothe the grass which is to-day in the field, and to-morrow is *cast into the oven*, how much more will he clothe you, O ye of little faith?"

When I recall the sight of a burning *tennûr*, I do not find it difficult to imagine what the old theologians meant by the "burning pit." The billows of black smoke, pierced at intervals by tongues of flame issuing from the deep hole, convert the chimneyless hut into an active crater. No one who has seen such a sight can fail to understand what the prophet Malachi meant when he exclaimed, "For, behold, the day cometh, that shall burn as an oven; and all the proud, yea, and all that do wickedly, shall be stubble." [1] And no one who has seen that little hut, virtually plastered with the blackest soot, can fail to understand the full meaning of that passage in the fifth chapter of the Book of Lamentations, the tenth verse, which says, "Our skin was black like an oven, because of the terrible famine."

A large baking is a source of pride as well as a means of security. A Syrian housewife is proud to have the oven all to herself for a whole day. It is a disgrace—nay, a curse—to have a small baking, or to buy bread in small quantity, "one weight" at a time. One of the terrible threats to Israel, recorded in the twenty-sixth chapter of the Book of Leviticus, the twenty-sixth verse, is this: "When I have broken the staff of your bread, ten women shall bake your bread in one oven, and they shall deliver you your bread again by weight: and ye shall eat and not be satisfied." My mother often admonished us to be thankful that we were not like those who had to buy their bread by weight— that is, in small quantities.

But this saying, "and they shall deliver you your bread again by weight," may mean also the weighing of the portions delivered to the various members of the family, in order that no one may receive more than any other, and that the scanty supply of food may be more carefully doled out. However, probably because no real famine ever occurred in Syria within my memory, I never knew of the actual resorting, within the family circle, to such severe restrictions in the distribution of the daily food. A similar practice, however, prevails among the Arab tribes in sharing their meager supply of water, while traveling in the desert. In order to insure equality, a pebble is placed in the bottom of a small wooden cup into which the water is poured. The draught which each traveler receives at long intervals is "the covering of the pebble," that is, only the quantity of water needed just to cover the pebble in the cup.

[1] Mal. iv: 1.

Chapter Three - "Compel Them to Come In"

The hospitality of Orientals is proverbial the world over. And while some Westerners have an exaggerated idea of Oriental generosity, the son of the East is not unjustly famous for his readiness to offer to wayfarers the shelter of his roof and his bread and salt. The person who fails to extend such hospitality brings reproach, not only upon himself, but upon his whole clan and town.

But whether hospitality is extended to strangers or to friends, it is the man who entertains, and not the woman. The invitation is extended in the name of the husband alone, or, if the husband is not living, in the name of the eldest son. In the case of a widow who has no male children, a man relative is asked to act as host. The man of the house should not allow a wayfarer to pass him without offering him a "morsel of bread to sustain his heart." So did Abraham of old extend hospitality to the three mysterious strangers who came upon him "in the plains of Mamre," as stated in the eighteenth chapter of Genesis, the second and following verses, "And he lift up his eyes and looked, and, lo, three men stood by him: and when he saw them, he ran to meet them from the tent door, and bowed himself toward the ground, and said, My Lord, if now I have found favor in thy sight, pass not away, I pray thee, from thy servant; ... and I will fetch a morsel of bread, and comfort ye your hearts: after that ye shall pass on."

How natural and how truly Syrian all this sounds! Sarah was not at all slighted because Abraham did not say, "Sarah and I will be glad to have you stop for lunch with us, if you can." On the contrary, she was greatly honored by not being mentioned in the invitation.

We have another striking illustration of this Syrian custom in the parable of the prodigal son, in the fifteenth chapter of St. Luke's Gospel. Here we are

69

told that, when the wayward boy returned to his father's house, desolate but penitent, it was the father who ran out to meet the son and "fell on his neck, and kissed him." It was the father who said to his servants, "Bring forth the best robe, and put it on him; and put a ring on his hand, and shoes on his feet; and bring hither the fatted calf, and kill it; and let us eat, and be merry." I know well that the mother of the prodigal could not have been less affectionate nor less effusive in her welcome to her poor son than his father was. But in harmony with the best traditions of the East, and without the least intention of slighting the good mother, the record takes no notice of her.

It should be stated here that the prominent mention in the Gospels of Mary and Martha as Jesus' friends and entertainers is due to the fact that to those women the Master was not merely a *guest*, but a *saint*, nay, the "promised One of Israel." As such Jesus was a privileged personage. Yet—and it is not at all strange in view of Oriental customs—Jesus took with him none of his women friends and disciples on such great occasions as the Transfiguration and the Last Supper.

To extend hospitality in genuine Syrian fashion is no small undertaking. Brevity on such occasions is the soul of stinginess. Oriental effusiveness and intensity of speech are never more strenuously exercised than at such times. The brief form of the American invitation, "I should be pleased to have you dine with us, if you can," however sincere, would seem to an Oriental like an excuse to escape the obligation of hospitality. Again, the ready acceptance of an invitation in the West would seem to the son of the East utterly undignified. Although the would-be guest could accept, he must be as insistent in saying, "No, I can't," as the would-be host in saying, "Yes, you must."

Approaching his hoped-for guest, a Syrian engages him in something like the following dialogue, characterized by a glow of feeling which the translation can only faintly reveal:— "Ennoble us [*sherrifna*] by your presence."

"I would be ennobled [*nitsherref*] but I cannot accept."

"That cannot be."

"Yea, yea, it must be."

"No, I swear against you [*aksim 'aleik*] by our friendship and by the life of God. I love just to acquaint you with my bread and salt."

"I swear also that I find it impossible [*gheir mimkin*] to accept. Your bread and salt are known to all."

"Yea, do it just for our own good. By coming to us you come to your own home. Let us repay your bounty to us [*fadhlek*]."

"*Astaghfero Allah* [by the mercy of God] I have not bestowed any bounty upon you worth mentioning."

Here the host seizes his guest by the arm and with an emphatic, "I *will not* let you go," pulls at him and would drag him bodily into his house. Then the guest, happy in being vanquished "with honor," consents to the invitation.

Do you now understand fully the meaning of the passage in the fourteenth chapter of Luke's Gospel? "A certain man made a great supper, and bade many ... and they all with one consent began to make excuse.... And the Lord said unto the servant, Go out into the highways and hedges, and *compel* them to come in, that my house may be filled." [1] So also did Lydia, "a seller of purple, of the city of Thyatira," invite the apostles, who had converted her to the new faith. In the sixteenth chapter of the Book of Acts, the fifteenth verse, Paul says, "And when she was baptized, and her household, she besought us, saying, If ye have judged me to be faithful to the Lord, come into my house, and abide there. *And she constrained us.*"

In the interior towns and villages of Syria the ancient custom still prevails that, when a stranger arrives in a town late in the day, he goes and sits in the "open space" (*saha*). While not designed to be so, this open space corresponds to the village common. In the English Bible it is called "the street." Streets, however, are unknown to Syrian towns. Sitting in the *saha*, the stranger is the guest of the whole village. The citizen who first sees such a wayfarer must invite him to his home in real Syrian fashion. Failing in this, he brings disgrace, not only upon himself, but upon the whole town. It is needless to say that no people ever rise to the height of their ideals, and that failure to be "given to hospitality" occurs, even in the East.

In the nineteenth chapter of the Book of Judges we have the record of a stranger who sat in the *saha* of a certain village, but was not offered the usual hospitality very readily. This man was a Levite, and, with his wife, servant, and a couple of asses, was on his way from Bethlehem "toward the side of Mount Ephraim." "And the sun went down upon them when they were by Gibeah, which belongeth to Benjamin. And they turned aside thither, to go in and to lodge in Gibeah: and when he went in, he sat him down in a street of the city; for there was no man that took them into his house to lodging. And, behold, there came an old man from his work out of the field at even.... And when he had lifted up his eyes, he saw a wayfaring man in the street of the city: and the old man said, Whither goest thou? and whence comest thou? And he said unto him, We are passing from Bethlehem-Judah toward the side of Mount Ephraim ... but I am now going to the house of the Lord; and there is no man that receiveth me to house."

And in order to add to the shame of the inhospitable village the stranger adds, "Yet there is both straw and provender for our asses; and there is bread and wine also for me, and for thy handmaid [the wife], and for the young man which is with thy servants: there is no want of any thing." What a rebuke to that community!

"And the old man said, Peace be with thee; howsoever let all thy wants lie upon me; *only lodge not in the street.* So he brought him into his house, and gave provender unto the asses: and they washed their feet, and did eat and drink."

The old man saved the name of the town.

One of the noblest and most tender utterances of Job is the thirty-second verse of the thirty-first chapter. Here the afflicted patriarch, in pleading his

71

own cause before the Most High, says, "The stranger did not lodge in the street, but I opened my doors to the traveller."

Syrian rules of hospitality make it improper for a householder to ask a guest who has suddenly come to him such a question as "Have you had your lunch?" before putting food before him. The guest, even though he has not had the meal asked about by the host, considers it below his dignity to make the fact known. Upon the arrival of such a visitor, the householder greets him with the almost untranslatable words, "*Ahlan wa sahlan.*" Literally translated, these words are "kindred and smooth ground"; which, elucidated further, mean, "You have come not to strangers but to those who would be to you as your kindred are, and among us you tread smooth and easy ground." And even while the guest is being yet saluted by the man of the house in the protracted manner of Oriental greeting, the good wife proceeds to prepare "a morsel" for the wayfarer, whatever hour of the day or night it may happen to be. The food then is placed before the guest and he is "compelled" to eat.

There is in the eleventh chapter of St. Luke's Gospel a parabolic saying which is uncommonly rich in allusions to Syrian home life. Beginning with the fifth verse we read: "And he said unto them, Which of you shall have a friend, and shall go unto him at midnight, and say unto him, Friend, lend me three loaves; for a friend of mine in his journey is come to me, and I have nothing to set before him; and he from within shall answer and say, Trouble me not: the door is now shut, and my children are with me in bed; I cannot rise and give thee?"

Here we have a man to whom a guest comes at midnight; he must set something before him, whether the wayfarer is really hungry or not. The host happens to be short of bread, and he sets out to borrow a few loaves. Owing to the homogeneous character of life in the East, borrowing has been developed there into a fine art. The man at the door asks for three loaves. Three of those thin Syrian loaves is the average number for one individual's meal. It was for this reason that the Master used this number in the parable, and not because that was all the bread the occasion required. For obvious reasons, the host needed to put before his guest more than the exact number of loaves necessary for one adult's meal. Perhaps because he is very sleepy, the man "within" runs counter to the best Syrian traditions in his answer. His excuse—that because the door is shut he cannot open it and accommodate his friend—has been a puzzle to a host of Western readers of the Bible. Could he not have opened the door? Or, as a certain preacher asked in my hearing, "Could it be possible that the man, because of fear of robbers in that country, had a sort of combination lock on his door which could not be easily opened?" The simple fact is that in Syria as a rule the door of a house is never shut, summer or winter, until bedtime. The words of my father and mother to me whenever they thought that I had "remained wakeful"—that is, "stayed up"—longer than I should after they had gone to bed,—"Shut the door and go to sleep,"—still ring in my ears. What the man "within" meant was, not that he could not open the door, but that at such a late hour, *after the door had been shut*, it was no time to call for such favors as the neighbor asked for.

"And my children are with me in bed." From this it may be inferred easily that individual beds and individual rooms are well-nigh unknown to the common people of Syria. The cushion-mattresses are spread side by side in the living room, in a line as long as the members of the family, sleeping close together, require. The father sleeps at one end of the line, and the mother at the other end, "to keep the children from rolling from under the cover." So the man was absolutely truthful when he said by way of an excuse, "My children are with me in bed."

In the remaining portion of this parable, as in that of the unrighteous judge, Jesus emphasizes, by commending to his disciples, the Syrian habit of importuning. "I say unto you, though he will not rise and give him, because he is his friend, yet because of his importunity he will rise and give him as many as he needeth." Again, the Master gives dignity and elevation to the common customs of his people by using them as means of approach to high spiritual ideals, when he says, "And I say unto you, ask and it shall be given you; seek, and ye shall find; knock, and it shall be opened unto you."

[1] Verses 16-23.

Chapter Four - Delaying the Departing Guest

The best rules of Syrian hospitality require that when a guest from a distant town makes it known what day he expects to take his leave, the host should do his best to trick his visitor into forgetfulness of the time set, or devise some other means to delay his departure as much as possible. On the day he wishes to depart, the wayfarer says to his host, "Your exceeding bounty has covered me, far above my head; may God perpetuate your house and prolong the lives of your dear ones. May He enable me some day to reward you for your boundless generosity. And now I who have been so immersed in the sea of your hospitality [*baher karamek*] beg you to permit me to depart." Then the host, confessing his unworthiness of such praise and manifesting great surprise at the sudden announcement, begs his guest to "take no thought of departing." The guest insists that he "must go," even though he could stay. The host says, "Stay, I pray you [*betrajjak*], until you partake of our noon meal; then you may depart." After the noon meal the host says, "I beg you to consider that the day is already far spent, and your journey is long, and the road is dangerous for night travel. Tarry until the morrow, and then go." The same performance takes place on the morrow, and perhaps another morrow, until the guest prevails.

In the nineteenth chapter of the Book of Judges, in the story of the Levite mentioned above, we have a fine example of a generous Syrian host. His words are so much like those I often heard spoken in Syria on such occasions that it makes me feel homesick to read them. The ancient Bethlehemite was entertaining his son-in-law, who had stayed with them three days, the traditional length of such a visit in the East. So the record says: "And it came to pass on the fourth day, when they arose early in the morning, that he rose up to depart: and the damsel's father said unto his son-in-law, Comfort thine heart with a morsel of bread, and afterward go your way. And they sat down, and did eat and drink both of them together; for the damsel's father had said unto the man, Be content, I pray thee, and tarry all night, and let thine heart be merry. And when the man rose up to depart, his father-in-law urged him: therefore he lodged there again. And he rose early in the morning on the fifth day to depart: and the damsel's father said, Comfort thine heart, I pray thee. And they tarried until afternoon, [1] and they did eat both of them. And when the man rose up to depart, ... his father-in-law, the damsel's father, said unto him, Behold, now the day draweth toward evening, I pray you tarry all night: ... lodge here, that thine heart may be merry; and to morrow get you early on your way, that thou mayest go home. But the man would not tarry that night, but he rose up and departed."

When an honored guest takes his departure, as a mark of high regard his host walks with him out of town a distance the length of which is determined by the affectionate esteem in which the host holds his visitor. At times we walked for a whole hour with our departing guest, and desisted from going farther only at his most urgent request. So in the eighteenth chapter of the Book of Genesis we are told that Abraham's guests "rose up from thence, and looked toward Sodom: and Abraham went with them *to bring them on the way.*" The English phrase, however, "to bring them on the way," falls far short of expressing the full meaning of the term *shy-ya'*.

Pilgrimages to holy places and fraternal feasts—such as are enjoyed on betrothal occasions, weddings, baptisms of children, and great holidays—are practically the only occasions the common people of Syria have to bring them together. On such occasions the guests are invited in families; therefore the number of those who come to the feast is never exactly known in advance. The food is served in large quantities, but not in such great variety as in the West. The table appointments are very simple. There are no flowers, no lace doilies, nor the brilliant and sometimes bewildering array of knives, forks, and spoons which grace an American host's table on such festive occasions. The guests sit close together on the floor, about low tables, or trays, and eat in a somewhat communistic fashion from comparatively few large dishes. If twenty guests are expected, and thirty come, they simply enlarge the circle, or squeeze closer together. Their sitting so close to one another makes the "breaking of bread together" for these friends more truly fraternal.

In the third chapter of St. Mark's Gospel, the twentieth verse, the writer speaks of the large concourse of people who followed Jesus and his disciples into a certain house. He tells us that "the multitude cometh together again, so that they *could not so much as eat bread.*" The cross-reference in the Bible points to the sixth chapter of the same Gospel, the thirty-first verse, where it is said, "For there were many coming and going, and they *had no leisure so much as to eat.*" My opinion is that the two occasions are not the same, therefore the reference is incorrect. The first passage alludes to the fact that although, owing to the very simple table appointments among the common people of Syria, only *little space* is required for one to eat his dinner, the crowd was so dense that not even such space was available. The second passage points to the fact that the Master's audience was a stream of people "coming and going" so that *his disciples* had not leisure enough to eat. The preceding verse and the first half of the verse just quoted say: "And the apostles gathered themselves together unto Jesus, and told him all things, both what they had done, and what they had taught. And he said unto them, Come ye yourselves apart into a desert place, and rest a while." The remainder of the verse gives the reason why Jesus felt so concerned about his fatigued and hungry disciples, by saying, "For there were many coming and going, and they [the disciples] had no leisure so much as to eat." The Syrian feels satisfied even on ordinary occasions when he can secure one or two loaves of the thin bread he habitually eats, and a few olives, or some other modest delicacy, for what the Americans would call a "lunch." He needs neither a table nor even a "lunch counter" to facilitate his eating. He can perform that essential function sitting down on the floor with his legs folded under him, standing up, or even walking, as well as seated at a table. In view of all this there is no little significance in the saying of the Gospel writer, "And the multitude cometh together again, so that they *could not so much as eat bread.*"

In several places in the Gospels reference is made to Jesus' "sitting at meat." [2] The marginal note in the Revised Version gives the word "recline" as the real equivalent of the original Greek term which is rendered "sit" in the text. This, no doubt, is correct, so far as the original text is concerned, but the reference is to a Greek and not to a Syrian custom. The Greeks were in the habit of reclining on couches while eating, and it is not at all improbable that certain wealthy Orientals imitated this custom in the time of Christ, as certain wealthy Syrian families of the present time imitate European customs. But I fail to find, either within my own experience, or in the traditions and literature of Syria, that reclining at the table was ever countenanced as at all a proper posture; certainly never among the common people of which the Master was one. To sit erect on the floor at the low table, with the legs either folded under the body, or thrown back as in the act of kneeling, is the seemly (*laiyik*) posture, which is ever sung in Arabic poetry. In this we were instructed from childhood. On unusual occasions, such as those of sorrow or great joy, friends might rest their heads on one another's shoulders, or breasts, as John did at the Last Supper, but these are rare exceptions. Good breeding and "reverence for the food" require the sitting erect at meat.

Certain commentators have found the reference to the habit of reclining at meat very serviceable in explaining Mary's act of anointing Jesus' feet with nard, as he sat at supper at her home in Bethany. In the twelfth chapter of the

Gospel of John, the third verse, it is said: "Then took Mary a pound of ointment of spikenard, very costly, and anointed the feet of Jesus, and wiped his feet with her hair." A similar incident is mentioned also in the seventh chapter of Luke, the thirty-sixth and following verses: [3] "And one of the pharisees desired him that he would eat with him. And he entered into the pharisee's house, and sat down to meat. And behold, a woman which was in the city, a sinner; and when she knew that he was sitting at meat in the pharisee's house, she brought an alabaster cruse of ointment, and standing behind at his feet, weeping, she began to wet his feet with her tears, and wiped them with the hair of her head, and kissed his feet, and anointed them with the ointment." The explanation is that it was convenient for the woman to wash and anoint Jesus' feet in this manner, because he was *reclining* on a couch.

What I am certain of is that the couch or any elevated seat is not at all necessary in such cases. Whenever an Oriental indulges in the practice of washing his feet he sits on the floor, as is his custom, and lifts the feet into the basin of water. This is the only way I ever knew in my old home, and it is no less effective than is the more "scientific" way of the West. King James's Version renders the passage a little more difficult by giving greater definiteness to the woman's position at Jesus' feet. While the Revised Version says, "And standing behind at his feet," the older Version says, "And stood behind *him*," etc. Yet even here the couch affords no greater advantage than the floor, because by folding the legs under the body, the feet are partially visible under the knee joints and could be touched from behind, and in the case of a kneeling posture, the feet may be easily reached from that direction. [4] However, it should be borne in mind here that the real significance of the entire passage is to be found, not in the woman's physical but spiritual act. It was her spirit of love and devotion to the Master, and, in the case of her who was a "sinner," her profound repentance and deep humility in touching Jesus' feet in this manner, which immortalized her act in the Scriptures. To the Orientals the feet are unclean in a ceremonial sense; they are not "honorable" members of the body; therefore to touch them in an act of devotion marks the deepest depth of humility. It was in this sense that Jesus humbled himself as an example to his disciples by washing their feet.

But objections may be made to the foregoing explanation on the ground that reclining at meat is mentioned in one of the most ancient books in the Old Testament, and which cannot be ascribed to the influence of Greek thought. In the sixth chapter of the Book of Amos, the third and fourth verses, it is said, according to the Revised Version: "Ye that put far away the evil day, and cause the seat of violence to come near; that lie upon beds of ivory, and *stretch themselves upon their couches, and eat the lambs out of the flock, and the calves out of the stall*." To some writers there is here a direct reference to the habit of reclining on couches while eating. But a careful study of the passage will show that its construction does not warrant such a conclusion. The passage cannot be made to read, "Ye ... that stretch themselves upon their couches *and eat*." The Hebrew word *weaukhalim* may mean, in this connection, "while eating," or, "and the eaters,"—those that eat. The rendering of the Arabic, which is a close kin of the Hebrew, is, "Ye ... who lie upon beds of ivory, and who are stretched on cushions [*fûrsh*], *and who eat lambs*," and so forth. Here it may easily be seen that the passage gives the theory of reclining at meat no real support, and the table customs of Syria past and present oppose any effort to force the passage to yield such a meaning. In his scathing condemnation of those who rolled in luxury and forgot God and his people, the prophet mentioned contemptuously the ease and the feasting of those whose life should have been more productive of good. He might have said, "Ye who lie on couches, and sing idle songs, and drink wine," as fittingly as, "Ye who lie on couches, and who eat lambs and calves."

[1] The more accurate rendering of this sentence in the Revised Version is, "And tarry ye until the day declineth." In the hot season a good excuse to delay a departing guest is to beg him to wait until the cool late afternoon, "The decline of the day [*assar*]."

[2] Matt. xxvi: 7, 20; John xii: 2.
[3] The Revised Version.
[4] As has already been mentioned, the common people of Syria wear no shoes in the house.

Chapter Five - Family Feasts

Of the feasts which are considered more strictly family affairs, I will speak of two which live in my memory clothed with romantic charms. The one is that which we enjoyed at the "killing of the sheep." As a rule every Syrian family fattens a sheep during the summer season. The housewife feeds the gentle animal by hand so many times during the day and so many during the night, until he is so fat that he "cannot rise from the ground." No person is expected to speak of this sheep or touch him without saying, "The blessing from God" (be upon the lamb). Oh, if I could but feel again the thrilling joy which was always mine when, as a small boy, I sat beside my mother and rolled the small "morsels" of mulberry and grape-leaves, dipped them in salted bran water, and handed them to my mother to feed the "blessed sheep"!

Early in the autumn came the time for "killing." Wherever my father was, he came home, for the father of the household must kill the sheep. As a rule the blood of the animal was shed upon the threshold—a custom which echoes the ancient Semitic practice of thus honoring the household god. Now, however, perhaps for sanitary reasons, the sheep is killed a short distance from the door. The solemnity of the act robbed it for us of its cruelty. On the day of "killing" we sharpened the knives, crushed the salt in the stone mortar, and fed the sheep only sparingly. As the day began to decline the animal was "led to the slaughter," and laid gently on the ground, as the ancient sacrifice was laid before the Lord. My father, holding with his left hand the animal's head, made the sign of the cross with the knife on the innocent throat, and, in the name of God, slew the sheep.

The fact that many householders in a community "kill the sheep" on the same day makes the occasion a reproduction of the night of the exodus from Egypt. In the twelfth chapter of the Book of Exodus, the third and sixth verses, Jehovah speaks to Moses concerning Israel, saying, "In the tenth day of this month they shall take to them every man a lamb, according to the house of their fathers, a lamb for an house.... And ye shall keep it up until the fourteenth day of the same month: and the whole assembly of the congregation of Israel shall kill it in the evening."

With a few intimate friends we feasted at the killing of the sheep, and then cut the red meat in small pieces "the size of a fledgeling's head," fried it in the fat, and sealed it in glazed earthen jars for our winter use.

The other most joyous feast was that of the *Marafeh*—the carnivals which precede the Great Lent. For about two weeks before Lent begins, the Christians of the East give themselves over to feasting. The dish which is a great favorite on this occasion is called *kibbey*. It is made of meat and crushed wheat. The meat is "beaten" in a stone mortar, with a large wooden masher, until it is reduced to a very fine pulp. Then the crushed wheat, soaked in cold water, is mixed with the meat, together with a generous supply of spices and salt. The whole mixture is then "beaten" together so thoroughly that when rightly done it resembles a lump of dough.

The writer of the Book of Proverbs, with characteristic Syrian intensity, alludes to the process of *kibbey*-making in one of his assaults upon "the fool." In the twenty-second verse of the twenty-seventh chapter he says, "Though thou shouldest bray a fool in a mortar among wheat with a pestle, yet will not his foolishness depart from him."

Be that as it may, the craving of a Syrian for *kibbey* (and I fully know whereof I speak) makes the craving of a Bostonian for baked beans and fishballs for a Sunday breakfast pale into insignificance.

During *Marafeh* friends and neighbors feast together until the last night that precedes the beginning of Lent. The feast of that night is one of family solemnity, upon which no outsiders may intrude. The members of the family come together to eat the last feast and drink their cup of wine before entering upon the solemn period of self-denial, fasting, and prayer. As at the ancient sacrificial feasts, all the members of the family must be present. It was this very custom which afforded Jonathan the excuse to send his beloved friend David away from King Saul's court, and thus save him from the murderous design which that monarch had against the son of Jesse. So it was when the suspicious Saul asked his son, "Wherefore cometh not the son of Jesse to meat, neither yesterday nor to-day?" Jonathan answered Saul, "David earnestly asked leave of me to go to Bethlehem: and he said, Let me go, I pray thee; for our family hath a sacrifice in the city; and my brother, he hath commanded me to be there." [1]

On that solemnly joyous evening my mother spreads the feast, and with most tender and pious affections my parents call their sons and daughters to surround the low table. My father pours the wine. To us all the cup is symbolic of sacred joy. Holding the cup in his hand, my father leans forward and says to my mother, "May God prolong your life and grant you the joy of many returns of this feast!" And to us, "May your lives be long; may we be granted to drink the cup at your weddings; may God grant you health and happiness and many future feasts!" We all answer, "May your drinking be health and happiness and length of days!" My mother, after wishing my father the blessings he wished for her, and imploring the Most High to bless and keep him "over our heads," drinks next. Then the wine is passed to every one of us. "Drink ye all of it" is my father's command; for who can tell whether the family circle shall remain unbroken until the Easter festival? Not a trace of the feast is kept in the house until the morrow. What is not eaten is burned or thrown away, for on the next day no meat, eggs, or milk is permitted to the faithful. Wine also is not supposed to be indulged in during Lent, until the Easter bell heralds the tidings of the Resurrection.

So did the Master speak to his disciples on the eve of his suffering. In the twenty-sixth chapter of St. Matthew's Gospel we read, "And he took the cup, and gave thanks, and gave it to them, saying, Drink ye all of it.... But I say unto you, I will not drink henceforth of this fruit of the vine, until that day when I drink it new with you in my Father's kingdom."

Thus from the simplest conception of bread as a means to satisfy physical hunger to the loftiest mystic contemplation of it as a sacramental element, the Orientals have always eaten bread with a sense of sacredness. "Bread and salt," "bread and wine," "Christ the bread of life," "For we, being many, are one bread," "Give us this day our daily bread," these and other sayings current in the Bible and in Oriental speech all spring from the deepest life of the ancient East.

And the sacredness of this common article of food has been of most inestimable value to Oriental peoples. In the absence of other means of social cohesion, and the higher civil interests which bind men together, it has been a great blessing indeed to those much-divided Orientals to find peace and security in the simple saying, "There is bread and salt between us."

[1] 1 Sam. xx: 27-29.

Part Four - Out in the Open

Chapter One - Shelter and Home

Some one has said that the ancient Israelites called God a "shelter" and a "refuge," and not a "home," because for the most part the Syrians lived out of doors. All the habitation an Israelite needed was a shelter from the storm and a refuge from the enemy. Hence the prayer of the Psalmist: "For thou hast been a shelter for me, and a strong tower from the enemy," [1] and the prophecy of Isaiah, the fourth chapter and the sixth verse, according to the Revised Version: "And there shall be a pavilion for a shadow in the day-time from the heat, and for a refuge and for a covert from storm and from rain."

The assertion that the Syrian, both ancient and modern, lives for the most part out of doors is substantially correct. The long and rainless summers, the almost exclusively agricultural and pastoral life of the people, outside the few large cities, and the primitive modes of travel, enable the Syrian to live his life out in the open. His one-story house, consisting of one or two rooms very simply furnished, conveys the impression that it is only an emergency shelter. Yet that artless structure and the living "close to nature" have proved so agreeable and so satisfactory to the people of the East as to defy the forces of evolution. Certainly the continuance of that simple environment, "from age to age the same," indicates that in the universal scheme of things evolution is not altogether compulsory. Man can, if he chooses, stand still, and live somewhat comfortably by simply repeating the past.

To the Oriental life is neither an evolution nor an achievement, but an inheritance. To his passive yet poetical mind the ancient landmarks possess enchanting sentimental value. The thought of the same modes of life linking fifty centuries together appeals powerfully to his imagination. It spells security, and establishes confidence in the laws of being, at least to old age.

However, it should not be inferred from the foregoing that the Syrian thinks lightly of his humble home. No; he is a passionate lover of it, and associates with it the deepest joys and sorrows of life. But he does not have for his abode the two designations "house" and "home," which prevail in the West. The Hebrew word *bayith* and the Arabic *bait* mean primarily a "shelter." The English equivalent is the word "house." The richer term, "home," has never been invented by the son of Palestine because he has always considered himself "a sojourner in the earth." His tent and his little house, therefore, were sufficient for a shelter for him and his dear ones during the earthly pilgrimage. The word which is translated "home" in about forty places in the English version of the Bible does not differ in the original from the word "house," which is found in about three thousand five hundred passages in the

Bible. The terms "tent," "house," "place of residence," and the phrases, "to go to his kindred," "to return to his place," etc., are all translated "home," and "go home."

To the Oriental the word "house" is very precious. It means the place of safe retreat (malja). And it is this word which he uses in speaking of God as his protector. It means more than "shelter." It is a place of protection and comfort. The word "refuge" is a more suitable equivalent. In that contentious East we always thought of a safe refuge in time of trouble. Every family of the common people "belonged" to some powerful lord who was its refuge in time of danger. He was strong, rich, compassionate. He protected his own. How much stronger, richer, and more compassionate, therefore, is the Lord of Hosts! The needy and much terrified Oriental discovered long ago the frailty of all earthly shelters. The King of Kings and the Lord of Hosts was his never-failing refuge. The trustful contemplation of God as an ever-present helper has steadied the faltering steps of countless generations. "The Lord is my rock, and my fortress, and my deliverer; my God, my strength, in whom I will trust; my buckler, and the horn [2] of my salvation, and my high tower." [3] "God is our refuge and strength, a very present help in trouble. Therefore will not we fear, though the earth be removed, and though the mountains be carried into the midst of the sea." [4]

Is it not really worth while to fear and to suffer, if by so doing one is brought so close to God? The writer of the one hundred and nineteenth Psalm had the world in his debt when he turned his inward vision toward the Most High and prayed: [5] "It is good for me that I have been afflicted; that I might learn thy statutes. The law of thy mouth is better unto me than thousands of gold and silver." And who can estimate the debt which humanity owes to the Sufferer of Calvary?

[1] Ps. lxi: 3.
[2] The "horn" symbolizes strength.
[3] Ps. xviii: 2, 3.

[4] Ps. xlvi: 1, 2.
[5] Ps. cxix: 71, 72.

Chapter Two - Resigned Travelers

Traveling by the "Twentieth Century, Limited," is fast transit; but, excepting in case of a wreck, the trip is devoid of incident. The mechanical perfection of the conveyance, and the infallibility of the time-table reduce journeying to transportation. There is no girding of the loins, no pilgrim's staff, no salutations by the way and no wayfarer's song. The journey is not humanized by the tender care for the camel, the mule, and the ass, nor are the hunger and thirst satisfied by the breaking of bread beside the lonely springs of water.

The terrors and triumphs of St. Paul in his "journeyings often, in perils of waters, in perils of robbers, in perils by mine own countrymen, in perils by the heathen, ... in weariness and painfulness, in watchings often, in hunger and thirst, ... in cold and nakedness," [1] are all to the modern Western traveler echoes of a remote past.

But such are still the common experiences of the sons of the East. One of the heroic wedding songs which was much in vogue in my boyhood days was this (addressed to the bride): "Thy father, O beauteous one, journeyed to Damascus alone!" Previous to the introduction of the railway train, which now runs between Beyrout and Damascus, the journey from my home town to the latter city consumed two days. In those days, as is still the case in many parts of Syria, men traveled in large groups for mutual protection from the "hidden dangers of the way," and he who journeyed to the ancient city alone was proclaimed hero. My memories of the tales of adventure which I heard the men relate are very thrilling. Tales of encounters with robbers, battles with snakes and wild beasts, suffering from the insufficiency of "the food for the way" (*zad*) and the thirst occasioned by the early "failure," that is, the drying up, of springs of water which had been thought to be still flowing.

Only those who have traveled under such circumstances can fully appreciate the promise given in the fifty-eighth chapter of Isaiah, the eleventh verse, "And the Lord shall guide thee continually, and satisfy thy soul in drought, and make fat [2] thy bones: and thou shalt be like a watered garden, and like a spring of water, *whose waters fail not.*"

This recalls forcibly to my mind the occasions when in our travels in the late summer we would stand at the parting of two roads and wonder which one to take. The opinion of the more experienced men in the party, that the spring of water on one of those roads was likely to be dry in that season of the year, always turned our steps in the other direction. In that thirsty land such a possibility could not be safely ignored. In those long summer days, when the mouth of the traveler on the dusty roads of Syria "turns bitter from the thirst," the arrival at a spring which had "failed" is almost a tragic experience. Hence it is that the "springs of water" are one of the precious promises of the Bible, and their failure was one of the fearful threats.

It was indeed a call to his disciples to make the great renunciation when Jesus sent them out to preach the glad tidings of the kingdom which was "at hand," with the command, "Provide neither gold, nor silver, nor brass in your purses, nor scrip for your journey, neither two coats, neither shoes, nor yet staves." [3] So far as the comforts and protection that earthly things can give, those disciples were sent out perfectly helpless. The Master's programme for those disciples is just the antithesis of that which an ordinary Oriental traveler follows.

No traveler in the interior of Syria ever starts out on a journey, be it short or long, without *zad*. True, Syrian generosity to a wayfarer is to be depended upon, but the traditions of the country are that self-respect requires that a traveler shall provide himself with *zad*, and shall accept hospitality only as a last resort. The best etiquette requires that when a traveler is invited to another's table, he should take out his *zad* and place it before him. The host, on the other hand, positively refuses to allow his chance guest to eat of his own *zad*. The host removes the *zad* from the table, and either adds to it and gives it to the guest upon his departure or gives him a new *zad*. Without scrip, the traveler seems to himself to be utterly a dependent, a beggar, and not a guest.

"Put up a few loaves for *zad*," is the first thing said when a person is about to start out on a journey. The thin loaves are folded into small bundles, which may contain such delicacies as ripe black olives, cheese, boiled eggs, and figs conserved in grape molasses, and wrapped up in a large napkin, which the traveler ties around his waist, with the bread on the back. The bread is often carried in a leather bag (*jerab*). This is the "scrip" and "wallet" of the Gospel command. On a long journey, say of a day or more, the thin bread dries up and breaks into small pieces. A dry and crumby *zad* indicates a long journey. The Gibeonites certainly "did work wilily" when they used their dry and broken bread as a means to deceive Joshua. Although they were Israel's near neighbors, by carrying dry crumbs in their bags and saying to Joshua upon their arrival at his camp, "This our bread we took hot for our provision out of our houses on the day we came forth to go unto you; but now, behold, it is dry, and it is mouldy," [4] made him and "the princes of the congregation" believe that the wily travelers had come from a distant country. The English translation, however, by using the word "mouldy" introduces a foreign element into the text. In the dry climate of Palestine the bread does not get *mouldy* on a journey, but it dries up and crumbles into small fragments, as every Syrian knows. The Arabic version has it, "This our bread ... is now dry and in crumbs [*fetat*]."

"Provide neither gold, nor silver, nor brass in your purses." The original text has "girdles" instead of "purses." While traveling in the East we always carried our money in the girdle and only a few coins in the purse. The girdle of the present day is a stout woolen or cotton belt, which is called, in the vernacular Arabic, *kummer*. It is worn under the sash, and the longest specimen of it measures about five feet. It is double to the length of about thirty inches. The two folds are very securely sewed together at the edge, and only a small opening provided near the buckle, through which the money is inserted. The double part, containing the money, is first fastened around the waist by means of a short leather buckle, then the single part is wound over it. It may be seen here that in case of an encounter with robbers, the money cannot be snatched from its owner until he is completely subdued by his antagonist.

The common people of Syria speak of the *kummer* as of a man's financial strength. There are practically no "bank accounts." "How is the *kummer*?" means, "How do you stand financially?" To tap the *kummer* cheerfully indicates good circumstances. It is joy and glory for a youth when he reaches the age when he may have a *kummer*. The thrill of satisfaction which that possession gives still lingers with me. It was as much of a sign of maturity and independence for me to tap that Scriptural girdle which I wore, when I had money in it, as to swear by my newly sprouting mustache. It was my treasure!

From all this it may be noted that the Master's command, "Provide neither gold, nor silver, nor brass in your girdles," meant, not only to carry no money on their missionary journey, but to seek and *horde* no money. An Oriental's girdle is his bank.

The part of the command which says, "Neither two coats," means two changes of clothing. The thing sought here, however, as well as in the saying, "Neither shoes," is not the abandonment of the necessary wearing apparel, but willing self-denial.

"Nor yet staves." The staff, or the "stick of travel," is the symbol of journeying in Syria. There, *Elkeina el'asa* (rested the staff) means we reached the end of our journey. *El'asa* (staff) occupies a significant place in Syrian lore. It is difficult for me to imagine a Syrian starting on a journey without an *asa*. The Israelites were given explicit directions concerning their preparations for the journey on the eve of their exodus from Egypt. They were told [5] to eat the lamb of the passover "with your loins girded, your shoes on your feet, *and your staff in your hand.*"

In our travels in Syria the staff was to us a most valuable support in climbing the steep hills, crossing the streams of water, battling with snakes and ferocious dogs, and with highway robbers. "The staff is a companion" is a current saying in the land. The disciples were commanded in this manner to detach themselves from the material interests of this world, and to give themselves wholly to the preaching of the kingdom. In their need and in their weakness they were to be rich and strong through their vision of the eternal realities.

In the tenth chapter of St. Luke's Gospel, Jesus' commission to the disciples contains the command, "And salute no man by the way." It would seem strange, indeed, that those messengers of peace and good-will, who were being sent out to spread the leaven of friendliness and good cheer in the world, should be enjoined by their Master to salute no man by the way. But when it is known in what manner the Orientals salute one another on those weary journeys, the Gospel restriction will not seem so very strange. Wayfarers in the East do not content themselves with the severely brief Western salutation, "How d' you do; nice day," and then pass on. The Oriental salutation is a copious flow of soul, whose intimacy and inquisitiveness are quite strange to the mentality of the West.

When the ways of two travelers converge, or the one overtakes the other, and they decide to *yatrafeko* (be companion the one to the other) and "wear away the road in friendly speech," the salutation runs as follows:—

"*Allah y'atek el'afieh* [May God give you health and strength]."

"*Allah y'afie imrak* [May God refresh and strengthen your life]."

"Whence has your excellent presence [*heth-retek*] come, and whither are you facing?"

"From Nazareth have I come, and am facing towards Damascus."

"What is the precious name?"

"Your humble servant Mas'ud, son of Yusuf of the clan of Ayyub [Job]."

"*Wann'am, wann'am* [All honor, all honor]!"

"*Wann'am* to your excellent presence, and your respected clan!"

"What are your years?"

"My years, friend, are four and thirty."

"May your life be long and happy!"

"May Allah lengthen your days!"

"What children have you?" (It is taken for granted that a man of that age has been long since married.)

"Three sons in the keeping of God."

"Long life to them and health and happiness!"

"What men does your clan count?"

"We turn out *seb'een baroody* [seventy shotguns]."

"*Seb'een baroody*! Valiant men. What enemies have you in your native town?"

"Our chief enemy is the clan of Haddad. They turn out one hundred *baroody*, but whenever the iron gets hot [that is, whenever a fight occurs] we shatter their forces."

Thus the mutually complimentary conversation and the searching of hearts continue until each of the travelers is thoroughly informed concerning the personal, domestic, and social affairs of the other. The trade, the income, the profession, the cares and anxieties, and even the likes and dislikes of each are made known to the other before their ways part.

Hence the Master's command, "Salute no man by the way." Surely the intention was not to be rude and unfriendly to fellow travelers, but to be completely absorbed by the glorious message of the Gospel. The command was given because "the king's business required haste." Even an Oriental must quicken his pace when his mission is "to seek and to save that which was lost."

[1] 2 Cor. xi: 26, 27.

[2] The Arabic and the Revised Versions: "make strong."

[3] Matt. x: 9, 10.

[4] Joshua ix: 12.

[5] Exod. xii: 11.

Chapter Three - The Market Place

I cannot think of the market place in the East without at the same time thinking of the camel caravan. In many parts of Syria, the arrival of the caravan makes the market. *El-habbet* (the grain) is the chief commodity, and the camel is the chief carrier. In very recent years the railway train has to a certain extent taken from the camel his ancient occupation, but it has by no means completely supplanted the "ship of the desert."

The coming of camel caravans from the "land of the east" to our Lebanon town, laden with the "blessed grain," is one of my most enchanted memories of outdoor life in Syria. The sight of a train of camels, with their curved necks bridging the spaces between them, suggests to the beholder an endless line. It is not at all surprising to me to read the assertion of the writer of the seventh chapter of the Book of Judges, where he speaks of the Midianites and Amalekites, that "their camels were without number, as the sand of the seaside for multitude." It seems to me that it does not require more than a train of one hundred camels to convey the idea of endlessness.

At the first glimpse of the approaching caravan we boys would swarm to the *saha* (the open space) of the town. There the caravan unloads, and awaits the buyers of wheat. It makes me long for my early years when I read in the twenty-fourth chapter of the Book of Genesis the story of Abraham's servant when he journeyed to Mesopotamia. "And the servant took ten camels of the camels of his master and departed.... And he made his camels to kneel down without the city by a well of water at the time of the evening, even the time that women go out to draw water." It is decidedly thrilling to hear the cameleer say, *ich, ich, i—ch—ch!* and pull at the halter of his camel to make him "kneel." And, with a friendly roar, the great beast drops, first forward on his huge, thick, hardened knees, then comes down on his haunches, and then, swaying in all directions, like an island shaken by an earthquake, rests his enormous body on the ground.

"At the time of the evening [in the late afternoon], even the time that women go out to draw water," the camels are led to the fountains to be watered. The ancient writer's reference to "the time that women go out to draw water" is to a Syrian as definite as the reference to a Swiss clock. *Wakket elmeliah* (the time to fill the jars) is in the early morning and the late afternoon. For obvious reasons the women choose the "cool of the day" for carrying their heavy jars of water from the fountain to the house. The Syrian women have faithfully kept this custom from before the days of Abraham. And it is in the cool of the day that the cameleers also deem it best to water their precious animals. The women always view this event with disfavor. The thirsty camels completely drain the pond into which the surplus water of the slender fountain flows, and which the housewives put to other household uses than drinking. No doubt the ancient Israelitish women in certain sections of Palestine grumbled when the cameleers drew heavily out of the wells on which the home-makers depended entirely for their water supply.

But to us boys the occasion was festive. By bribing the cameleers with gifts of grapes, figs, raisins, or any other sweets, for which the craving of the Bedouins is proverbial, we were allowed to mount the camels and lead them to the water. It may be true, as some scholars assert, that the swaying walk of the camel first quickened the measured song of the Arab, but my first camel ride was anything but poetical. I had, upon the arrival of the caravan, smuggled from our store of raisins two large pocketfuls, the one with which to bribe the Bedouin to give me a ride, the other to eat while on the camel's back, like a gay rider. As I climbed confidently on the wooden saddle of the kneeling beast, the Arab, who was already devouring the raisins, stems and all, by the handful, gave the familiar signal, *tshew, tshew*, and instantly the thirsty camel rose and flew toward the fountain. I felt as if my brain was being torn off its base. I lost the sense of direction, and seemed to myself to be suspended between earth and heaven, tossed by violent winds. I screamed; but the Bedouin would not let me down until I promised him the other pocketful of raisins.

In Syria the *sûk* (market place) is more than a place of exchange of commodities. It is rather an occasion of varied business and social interests. The Oriental knows no business without sociability. His *dekkan* (store) is a gathering-place for friends, and a business transaction with him, especially in the interior of the country, is almost always preceded by a friendly visit with the customer. So the market is a place where the dignitaries of the town meet and exchange salutations and discuss various interests. The social nature of such occasions is indicated in Jesus' warning to his disciples, "Beware of the scribes, which love to go in long clothing, and *love salutations in the marketplaces.*" [1] Apparently those teachers of Israel were very frequent visitors at the markets, where men of all classes paid them the homage which their calling, if not their person, merited. In the past the Arab markets were also significant conventions of literary men, especially poets. Discussions of all sorts of subjects are carried on at the market. So it was in Athens in Paul's time, where he "disputed ... in the market daily with them that met with him." [2] And, of course, the children love to gather in the market place, play their pranks, and watch the interesting activities of their elders. It was to such a crowd of youngsters that Jesus likened the fickle and peevish men of his time. In the eleventh chapter of St. Matthew's Gospel, the sixteenth verse, he says, "But whereunto shall I liken this generation? It is like unto children sitting in the markets, and calling unto their fellows, and saying, We have piped unto you, and ye have not danced; we have mourned unto you, and ye have not lamented."

To my youthful mind the chief charm of the market place was the *keyyal* (measurer). The strong man who measured the wheat will live in my memory as long as life endures. He it is who gives the "good measure, pressed down, shaken together, running over." In Syria the custom is that every measure must run over. Friendship must forever be mixed with business. Liquid measures, also, of such things as milk and oil, must run over a little into the vessel of the buyer, for "with what measure ye mete, it shall be measured to you again." [3]

After the price has been agreed upon, the sturdy cameleer spreads his ample cloak on the ground and pours the golden grain in a heap upon it. The *keyyal* kneels by the little hillock of wheat, and, naming the Holy Name, thrusts the *midd* (a wooden measure) into the precious wheat. The grain is sacred; therefore, the language of the *keyyal* must be pious. As he tosses the first measure into the buyer's bag, or the skirt of his cloak, he says, "Blessing!" that means "One"; "From God" means "Two." Then the counting is continued in the ordinary language—three, four, and so on.

After it is first thrust into the heap of wheat, the *midd*, about half full, is whirled around on its bottom, lifted slightly from the ground and dropped several times. The *keyyal*, constantly repeating the number of the *midds* he has already measured, "lest he forget," pours the wheat into the measure with his hands, packs it down with his palms, and all his strength. He whirls the *midd* round again, shakes it, presses it, and again heaps the wheat, pyramid-like, above the rim. The circular shower of the golden grain falls gently over the edges. The artful *keyyal* pours small handfuls of wheat with his right hand into his left, which is formed into a funnel over the apex of the heaped *midd*, until the point is "as sharp as a needle's." Then with swift deftness, which elicits the admiration of the spectators, he lifts the heaped measure and tosses it into the bag, without allowing a single grain to fall outside.

With what telling effect and rich simplicity does the Master allude to this custom of measuring grain in the Eastern markets. In the sixth chapter of St. Luke's Gospel, the command and the promise are, "Give, and it shall be given unto you; good measure, pressed down, and shaken together, and running over, shall men give into your bosom." But the word "bosom" here somewhat weakens the sense of the text. I do not know why the English translators used it in place of the original word "lap." The Oriental does not carry grain in his *bosom*, but in the skirt of his ample garments, much as a woman carries things in the fold of her apron. Again the word "lap" is used here in another and a more significant sense. It is the symbol of plentifulness; just as the "bosom" is the symbol of affection. The generous measure, even though it be poured into one's bag, as a *blessing*, may be said to be given into his *lap*.

Here again, as in many other Scriptural passages, Jesus gives the ideal spiritual touch to the common things of life. Here an ordinary act is made the symbol of the fullness of the spiritual life. He whose life is like the divine Parent's life—a perpetual outgoing and an everlasting gift—shall never lack anything. Men will be taught by his generosity how to be generous themselves, and the divine Giver will give him of the fullness of his own life. There is no void which the divine life cannot fill, no need which it cannot meet, and no hunger which it cannot satisfy.

[1] Mark xii: 38.   [2] Acts xvii: 17.   [3] Matt. vii: 2.

Chapter Four - The Housetop

While a caravan of camels needs no other means than its own majestic appearance to herald its arrival into a town, muleteer merchants shout their wares from the housetop. Upon the arrival of a muleteer into the *saha* of the town with a load of lentils, potatoes, apricots, or any other commodity, he "drops the load" from the animal's back onto the ground, and goes upon the roof of the nearest house and proclaims his wares at the top of his voice, in prolonged strains. To reach the flat earthen roof of the one-story Syrian house needs no extension ladder. It is so easily and quickly reached by the few rough stone steps in the rear of the house that Jesus, in speaking of the incredibly swift coming of the "end" in the twenty-fourth chapter in St. Matthew's Gospel, says, "Let him which is on the housetop not come down to take any thing out of his house." So sudden was to be the consummation of the Eternal's design, "because iniquity shall abound, and the love of many shall wax cold," that even the short distance between the housetop and the ground could not be safely traversed by those who cared for earthly possessions.

The ease with which the roof of an ordinary Syrian house is reached accounts also for the carrying of the man who was "sick of the palsy" upon the housetop. The account in the second chapter of St. Mark's Gospel, the third and fourth verses, runs, "And they came unto him, bringing one sick of the palsy, which was borne of four. And when they could not come nigh unto him for the press, they uncovered the roof where he was; and when they had broken it up [the Arabic, "broken through"], they let down the bed wherein the sick of the palsy lay."

This account describes perfectly the process of making an opening in a Syrian roof.

In St. Luke's Gospel, however, the statement is: [1] "And when they could not find by what way they might bring him in because of the multitude, they went upon the housetop, and let him down through the *tiling* with his *couch* into the midst before Jesus." The coloring here is decidedly Roman and not Syrian. The writer of Luke was a Latin Christian. He related the incident in terms which were easily understood by his own people. The Syrians never covered their roof with tiles nor slept on couches. Mark's account speaks of uncovering the *roof* and letting down the *bed*. The Syrian roof is constructed as follows: The main timbers which carry the roof covering are laid across, horizontally, at intervals of about two to three feet. Crosswise over the timbers are laid the *khasheb* (sticks long enough to bridge the spaces between) quite close together. Over the *khasheb* reeds and branches of trees and thistles are laid, and the whole is covered with about twelve inches of earth. The dirt is rolled down by a stone roller and made hard enough to "shed water." In many houses during the summer season an opening, called *qafa'a*, is made in the roof for the purpose of letting down the grain and other provisions which are dried in the sun on the housetop. The space between the timbers admits easily the large basket called *sell*, which is as big around as a bushel basket.

Now, those who let down the palsied man either made an entirely new opening in the roof, or simply extended the *qafa'a* enough to admit the unfortunate man in his folded quilt or thick cushion, tied by the four corners. And it was this which Jesus commanded him to carry, when he said to him, "Arise, and take up thy bed, and walk." From the foregoing it may be seen that a couch could not have been so easily let down through the roof, nor *carried* by the newly healed man.

Sleeping on the housetop in the summer season is an Oriental custom the advantage of which the Occident has just "discovered." To use the roofs of high buildings in American cities as sleeping quarters is a "new" suggestion of that genius known as the "social reformer." To the ancient East, "there is nothing new under the sun." However, to dwell on the housetop is an expression which symbolizes desolation. Nevertheless the writer of Proverbs says: [2] "It is better to *dwell* in a corner of the housetop, than with a brawling woman in a wide house."

From the housetop the muleteer merchant shouts his wares; from the housetop men call one another for various purposes; from the housetop the *nowateer* (men appointed by the municipality to watch the vineyards) proclaim the names of trespassers; and from that elevation the special orders of the governor of the district are proclaimed to the populace. By night or by day, whenever we heard a voice calling from a housetop, we instinctively listened most intently in order to catch the message. The voice of the crier is so much like a distant, prolonged railway whistle that in my first few years in America, whenever I heard such a sound, especially in the night, I listened involuntarily, expecting to hear a message.

How often must Jesus have heard the free and full voice of the crier from the housetop! How it must have appealed to him as the very antithesis of the whisperings of fear, cowardice, and doubt, may be realized from his command to his disciples. In the tenth chapter of St. Matthew's Gospel we read Christianity's declaration of independence. Here the antagonism of the world is portrayed with complete fullness. "Behold, I send you forth as sheep in the midst of wolves." "Ye shall be hated of all men for my name's sake." "Fear them not ... for there is nothing covered, that shall not be revealed; and hid, that shall not be known." In the face of all hatred and danger and death the Master's command to those who carried the world-transcending message, the supreme treasure of time and eternity, was, "What I tell you in darkness, that speak ye in light: and what ye hear in the ear, that preach ye upon the housetop."

In the rainless Syrian summer the housetop is used for various household purposes. The grass which grows on the earthen roof, especially on its thick edges, withers early in the season. To this the Scripture alludes in several places where it speaks of the enemies of Israel as being "like the grass upon the housetops, which withereth afore it groweth up." In some cases the whole roof is plastered with clay mortar and used for drying grain, fruits, and vegetables. Also in the summer season the housetop is used for holding wedding festivities and funeral gatherings, which almost all the adult inhabitants of the town are supposed to attend. With solemn brevity does the prophet Jeremiah refer to this custom in the forty-eighth chapter, and the thirty-eighth verse. The more accurate rendering of the Revised Version is: "*On all the housetops* of Moab and in the streets thereof there is lamentation every where."

The custom of praying on the housetop, which has come down from the time when the Syrians worshiped the "hosts of heaven," still survives in the East. In the first chapter of the Book which bears his name, the prophet Zephaniah threatens with the awful retribution of Jehovah those who indulged in this practice. "I will also stretch out mine hand upon Judah, and upon all the inhabitants of Jerusalem; and I will cut off the remnant of Baal from this place ... and *them that worship the host of heaven upon the housetops.*" This custom survives in Syria, although much less extensively than in the past, and it is "the God of the whole earth" that is worshiped, and not the host of heaven. With much reverential regard I still remember an old neighbor of ours, a devout Maronite, a man who really feared God and worked righteousness, whose habit was to say his evening prayer upon the housetop.

Of all the rich treasures of our Scriptures, few perhaps are more precious and dearer to Christian hearts than the record of Peter's vision while in the city of Joppa, and which is so intimately associated with that low, flat, earthen Syrian roof. The tenth chapter of the Book of Acts hints at the broader and more profound spirit which had begun to agitate the inner life of the "very small remnant" of expectant souls in Israel. The wider horizon which the Christ of God had revealed to his Jewish disciples had engendered serious doubts in their minds with regard to the exclusive claims of Judaism to the blessings of the Messianic kingdom. The spirit of the Beatitudes and the Parables was resistlessly pressing the claims of all the eager Gentiles to a share in those blessings. No doubt the soul of Peter, the ultra-conservative disciple, was rent in twain and wavered in its allegiance between the old claims of a "chosen people" and the new vision of a universal kingdom founded on purity of heart and hunger and thirst after righteousness.

It would seem that while in such a state of mind, and after the Oriental custom, "Peter went up upon the housetop to pray about the sixth hour; [3] and he became very hungry, and would have eaten: but while they made ready, he fell into a trance, and saw heaven opened, and a certain vessel descending unto him, as it had been a great sheet knit at the four corners, and let down to the earth; wherein were all manner of four-footed beasts of the earth, and wild beasts, and creeping things, and fowls of the air. And there came a voice to him, Rise, Peter; kill, and eat. But Peter said, Not so, Lord; for I have never eaten any thing that is common or unclean. And the voice spake unto him the second time, What God hath cleansed, that call not thou common."

Peter obeyed. That Oriental, who was not afraid of the mystic revelations of God's designs took the lesson to heart. Presently we see this conservative Jew again at the home of Cornelius, the Roman, and hear him interpret his own vision. "Of a truth," he said to the Roman soldier, "I perceive that God is no respecter of persons: but in every nation he that feareth him, and worketh righteousness, is accepted with him." Here we have the sure basis of Christian unity and the unshaken foundation of a human commonwealth. "Other foundation can no man lay." When all the sects and nations who profess to be the followers of Jesus Christ respond to this Scriptural summons, and give decent burial to their divisive creeds, however "authoritative" they might think them to be, then will the world have valid reason to expect swords to be beaten into ploughshares, and to hope for the coming of God's kingdom upon the earth.

[1] Luke v: 19.,   [2] Prov. xxi: 9.

[3] The noon hour, according to Oriental calculation: Timepieces are set at twelve, at sunset. Six o'clock is the hour of midnight and midday. The time kept by Western peoples is known in Syria as *affrenje*. So the laborers who came to work at "the eleventh hour," as it is mentioned in Matthew, the twentieth chapter, and the ninth verse, came one hour before sunset.

Chapter Five - The Vineyards and the Fields

From time immemorial the vine and the fig tree have been the Oriental's chief joy. Together with their actual value they possessed for him a sacred symbolic value, especially the vine. The fullness and sweetness of their fruits symbolized the joys of the kingdom of heaven. The mystery of the wine cup, which the world has so sadly vulgarized, remains very sacred to the Oriental. Christ used "the fruit of the vine," or, as the Arabic version has it, the *yield* of the vine,—meaning the wine, and not grapes,—as the visible means of spiritual communion. In the fifteenth chapter of St. John's Gospel the Master says, "I am the vine, ye are the branches." This usage was no doubt extant in the East before Christ. The vine, as a symbol of spiritual as well as physical family unity, is spoken of in the Old Testament. Israel's was Jehovah's vine. "Thou hast brought a vine out of Egypt" is the plaintive cry of the writer of the eightieth Psalm: "thou hast cast out the heathen, and planted it. Thou preparest room before it, and didst cause it to take deep root, and it filled the land.... Return, we beseech thee, O God of hosts: look down from heaven, and behold, and visit this vine; and the vineyard which thy right hand hath planted."

We always thought and spoke of the Church as "the vine which God has planted." The chanting of the foregoing words of the Psalmist by our priest of the Greek Orthodox Church, with his hand uplifted over the solemnly silent congregation, remains one of the most beautiful memories of my youth. We spoke also of the family as a vine. One of the tenderest passages in the whole Bible is the third verse of the one hundred and twenty-eighth Psalm: "Thy wife shall be as a fruitful vine by the sides of thine house: thy children like olive plants round about thy table."

"They shall sit every man under his vine and under his fig tree; and none shall make them afraid," [1] is Micah's vision of peace and security. To a Syrian in America the reading of this passage is strongly conducive to homesick-

92

ness. To sit in the luxuriant shade of the fig tree was a daily blessing to us in the summer season. It must have been in that season of the year that Jesus first met Nathanael. In the first chapter of St. John's Gospel we read: "Jesus saw Nathanael coming to him, and saith of him, Behold an Israelite indeed, in whom is no guile! Nathanael saith unto him, Whence knowest thou me? Jesus answered and said unto him, Before that Philip called thee, *when thou wast under the fig tree, I saw thee.*"

I have no doubt that Nathanael's habit of sitting under the fig tree was one of the characteristics which made him "an Israelite indeed."

The wine press is an ancient landmark in Syrian life, and one of the most picturesque features of the Scriptures. The word "press" is likely to be misleading in this mechanical age. The grapes are not *pressed* by any mechanical contrivance, but are trodden with the feet. Therefore, to the Orientals the wine press is *ma'sara* (squeezing place). The grapes are thrown in a heap in a stone-flagged enclosure about the size of an ordinary room, and trodden by the men in their bare feet. Much gayety characterizes the *ma'sara* season. The work is carried on day and night until all the grapes which had been gathered by the various families for the *ma'sara* are converted into wine and molasses. The quaint songs and stories which I always loved to hear the "treaders" exchange, as they walked back and forth over the grapes, come to me now like the echoes of a remote past. And as I recall how at the end of a long "treading" those men came out with their garments spattered with the rich juice of the grapes of Lebanon, the words of Isaiah—"Wherefore art thou red in thine apparel, and thy garments *like him that treadeth the wine fat?*" [2] —breathe real life for me.

But in this age of rampant microbiology I introduce this subject with at least an implied apology. The picture of men treading grapes in this manner and under such circumstances will not, I fear, appeal strongly to the æsthetic sense of my readers. Nevertheless, all the Scriptural wine, including the cup of the Last Supper, was produced in this way. To the Orientals the mystic fermentation and the fire purify the juice of the vine. The precious juice runs from the wide, stone-flagged enclosure into deep wells, where it is allowed to become *rawook* (clear juice). The fresh *rawook* is considered a delicious drink. One of Job's bitter complaints against those who oppressed the poor was that those unfortunates were made to "tread the wine presses, and *suffer thirst.*" [3] Having been allowed thoroughly to settle, the juice is then heated according as to whether the wine is to be "sweet" or "bitter." The longer the juice is boiled the sweeter the wine. Sweet wine is called *khemer niswani*(woman wine); the men, as a rule, preferring the "bitter" wine. In making molasses of the grape juice, fine white clay is scattered over the grapes before they are trodden, in order to hasten and insure a perfect settling of all the coarse organic matter while the juice is in the "clearing wells."

I often wonder whether it is because the memories of youth grow more romantic with the passing of the years, that the agricultural life of the Orient seems to me more poetical than that of the Occident, or whether it really is more enchanting. It seems to me that tools possess more charms than machinery does, and handwork of the more instinctive type is much more interesting than the carefully studied and designed task. The life of the American farmer is too intelligent to be romantic. There is so much in him of the agricultural college and the farm journal. No awful mysteries haunt his scientifically treated fields. Insect powders and the daily weather report and the market "quotations" arm him with forethought, and make of him a speculating merchant. The constant improvements of agricultural implements place a wide and ever-widening gulf between the American farmer and his forefathers.

Not so with the Syrian farmer. To this man life is not an evolution, but an inheritance. If the men who tilled Abraham's fields in Hebron should rise from the dead to-day, they would find that the four thousand years of their absence from the earth had effected no essential changes in the methods and means of farming in the "land of promise." They would lay their hand to the plough and proceed to perform their daily tasks, as though nothing had happened. A very few European ploughs are being tried in certain sections of Syria, but that is all.

The Syrian sower goes forth to sow with his long, primitive plough on his right shoulder, the yoke hanging from the left shoulder and the leather bag of seed strapped to his back. In his left hand he carries his long, hard, strong goad—the same as the one with which "Shamgar, son of Anath, slew of the Philistines six hundred men." Through this simple instrument he keeps in touch with his pair of oxen, or cows, which pace leisurely before him. The plough, which consists of two wooden beams joined together, measures about twelve feet in length. The quantity of wood in the Syrian plough makes plain the meaning of the passage in the story of the prophet Elisha, son of Shaphat. In the nineteenth chapter of the First Book of Kings, the nineteenth verse, we have the account of Elijah's first meeting with his successor Elisha, when he was ploughing in the field, "with twelve yoke of oxen before him, and he with the twelfth." So, when Elijah cast his mantle upon him, the son of Shaphat "took a yoke of oxen, and slew them, *and boiled their flesh with the instruments of the oxen*, and gave unto the people, and they did eat. Then he arose, and went after Elijah, and ministered unto him."

At the forward end the long plough is hooked to the yoke, and at the rear end joined to a cross-piece, whose upper extremity forms the *cabousa* (handle); and the lower holds the iron ploughshare. When he puts "his hand to the plough," he simply grasps the *cabousa* with his right hand while he wields the goad with his left. The uneven, stony ground and the lightness of the plough compel him to maintain a firm hold on it, and to look ever *forward*. In the ninth chapter of St. Luke's Gospel, the sixty-second verse, Jesus makes excellent use of this point when he says, "No man, having put his hand to the plough, and *looking back*, is fit for the kingdom of God."

The parable of the sower, in the thirteenth chapter of St. Matthew's Gospel, is a faithful picture of the environment of the farmer in the region of Galilee and Mount Lebanon. That primitive farmer does not sow his seed by means of "drills" in symmetrical rows. Out of his leathern seed bag he takes generous handfuls of grain and, "in the name of the bounteous God," he casts the blessed seed into the soil, and then "covers it" by ploughing. The bridle paths which wind through the fields, and the still narrower footpaths which the wayfarers make through those fields every season in taking "short cuts" on their weary journeys, provide ample chance for "some seeds" to fall "by the wayside," and be devoured by the fowls of the air. In certain sections of the country where I was brought up the "stony places" are the rule and the "good ground" the exception. So the seeds which "fell upon stony places" came up quickly "because they had no deepness of earth; and when the sun was up, they were scorched." There is another reason for this than the shallowness of the soil. The almost utter lack of rain in that country from April to October leaves no chance for seed cast into shallow soil to live long.

"And some fell among the thorns; and the thorns sprang up, and choked them." For this the Syrian farmer himself is largely to blame. He preserves the thorns for cattle feed and for fuel. Certain kinds of thorns, especially *bellan*, are used as fuel for summer cooking, which is done out of doors, and for baking at the *tennûr*. Other thorns are harvested, after the barley and wheat harvests, threshed, and stored for winter feed. In the sixth verse of the seventh chapter of the Book of Ecclesiastes the writer says, "For as the crackling of thorns under a pot, so is the laughter of the fool." The threshing of thorns is referred to in the Book of Judges, [4] where it says, "When the Lord hath delivered Zabah and Zalmunna into mine hand, then I will tear your flesh with the thorns of the wilderness and with briers." But here again the English translation fails to give an exact rendering of the text, although the marginal note replaces the word "tears" by the word "thresh." The Arabic version says, "I will *thresh* your flesh with the thorns and briers of the wilderness *with the threshing boards*," which is an exact picture of the treading of the oxen as they drag the threshing board over the thorns upon the threshing floor.

When a boy it was a great delight to me to wander in the wheatfields when the grain had just passed the "milk stage" and had begun to mature and harden. It is then called *fereek*, and is delicious to eat, either raw or roasted. I could subsist a whole day by plucking the heads of wheat, rubbing them in my hand and eating the fat, soft, fragrant grain. From time immemorial wayfarers in the East have been allowed to trespass in this manner, provided they carried no more grain away than that which they ate. In the twenty-fifth verse of the twenty-third chapter of the Book of Deuteronomy the reading of the Revised Version is, "When thou comest into thy neighbor's standing corn, then thou mayest pluck the ears with thine hand; but thou shalt not move a sickle unto thy neighbor's standing corn." It was the indulgence in this practice by the disciples, on the Sabbath, which formed the basis of the Pharisees' protest to Jesus to the effect that his followers dishonored the sacred day. In the sixth chapter of St. Luke's Gospel, the first verse, the Revised Version rendering of the text is, "Now it came to pass on a sabbath, that he was going through the grainfields and his disciples plucked the ears, and did eat, rubbing them in their hands." The protest of the guardians of Israel's law, and Jesus' answer in the verses which follow, give us another revelation of the Master's central thought and motive as a religious teacher; namely, that man's legitimate needs take precedence of all ecclesiastical formalities.

I do not believe any account of agricultural life in Syria should omit mentioning the plague which above all others strikes terror into the heart of the Eastern tiller of the soil. In his prayer at the dedication of the temple, Solomon mentions "blasting, mildew, locust, and caterpillar." [5] Of all those unwelcome visitors, the locusts are the most abhorred. I will give my impression of this pest in a quotation from my autobiography: [6]

One of the never-to-be-forgotten phenomena of my early years, a spectacle which the most extravagantly imaginative American mind cannot picture, was the coming of the locusts into our part of the country. If my memory serves me well, I was about twelve years old when my father and all his men, together with all the male population over fifteen, were impressed by the governor of our district to fight the devastating hosts of Oriental locusts. No one who has not seen such a spectacle and the desolation those winged creatures leave behind them can appreciate in the least degree the force of the saying of "The Lord God of the Hebrews" to Pharaoh, "If thou refuse to let my people go, behold, to-morrow I will bring the locusts into thy coasts." [7] For a few weeks before they deluged our district the news came with the caravans that the locusts were sweeping toward our region from the "land of the south." We youngsters did not know why our elders were so terror-stricken when they heard of it, until the scourge had come and gone.

It was a few weeks before the time of the harvest when the clouds of locusts enveloped our community. They hid the sun with their greenish-yellow wings, covered the trees and the ground, the walls and roofs of the houses, and dashed in our faces like flakes of snow driven by the wind. The utter hopelessness of the task which confronted our people and seemed to unite all classes in despair, assumed in my sight a very comic aspect, and converted the calamity into a holiday. It was so amusing to me to see our sedate aristocrats and old men and women join the youth and the common laborers in shouting, beating on tin cans, firing muskets, setting brush on fire, striking at the cursed insects with their hands, stamping them with their feet, and praying God to send "a strong wind" to drive the enemy of man away. Every *mutekellif* (payer of the toll-tax) had to fight the locusts for so many days or hire a substitute,

I do not clearly remember whether it was the beating on tin cans and howling of the people or the prayed-for "strong wind" that drove the merry locusts away. What I do remember is that when they did go away they left the land almost stripped clean of every green thing.

It was no vain threatening when the writer of Deuteronomy warned Israel, saying, "If thou wilt not hearken unto the voice of the Lord thy God, to observe to do all his commandments.... All thy trees and fruit of thy land shall the locust consume." [8]

[1] Mic. iv: 4.

[2] Is. lxiii: 2.

[3] Job xxiv: 11.

[4] Judges viii: 7.

[5] 1 Kings viii: 37.

[6] *A Far Journey*, page 109, etc.

[7] Exod. x: 40.

[8] Deut. xxvii: 15, 42.

Chapter Six - The Shepherd

"I am the good shepherd" is one of Jesus' most tender, most compassionate sayings. The first sixteen verses of the tenth chapter of St. John's Gospel, from which this saying comes, should be joined to the twenty-third Psalm. Notwithstanding the fact that John's words are tinged with Greek thought, as descriptive of shepherd life in the East, those two portions of Scripture belong together.

The various phases of shepherd life in Syria are indelibly printed in my memory. Our mountain village home was situated on the upper slope of a rather steep hill, at the base of which a thin stream flowed over its rocky bed. Across the narrow ravine, on the lower slope of another hill, just opposite our home, there were three sheep and goat folds. There for years I watched the shepherds and their flocks go out and come in, morning and evening, from early spring until late autumn, when the shepherds dismantled the folds by removing their thorny fences, pulled down their rude bowers, and led their flocks to the "lowlands," where they spent the short winter season. The wailing of Isaiah, in the twelfth verse of the thirty-eighth chapter (Revised Version), "My dwelling is removed and is carried away from me as a shepherd's tent," reminds me very strongly of the easy removal and complete disappearance of that temporary shelter, which I so often saw torn down and carried away.

While at work in the fields cutting stone for my father's building operations in various parts of Mount Lebanon, the shepherds were all around us. In those days I watched the shepherd lead his flock "into the waters of rest," or the restful, refreshing waters, which the English version renders "still waters." I watched him as, by inarticulate, deep, guttural sounds, whistling, certain characteristic words which the flock seemed to understand, and the flinging of pebbles or "smooth stones," such as those with which David smote Goliath, he guided, I might say invited, the "blessed creatures," into every nook and corner among the rocks where there was pasture. It was this solicitous watchfulness of the shepherd which the writer of the twenty-third Psalm had in mind when he said, "The Lord is my shepherd, *I shall not want*." In the heat of the day the shepherd made his flock "to lie down" in the pasture ground, and the "blessed ones," as the shepherd always calls his sheep and goats, would fold their nimble legs and lie down, singly and in small groups, a surpassing picture of contentment, trustfulness, and peace. They seemed to realize that although they were in the wilderness they had nothing to fear. For the loving shepherd, with his strong and heavy staff, was in their midst to ward off all danger from them.

The opening verses of the tenth chapter of the Gospel of John contain most significant allusions to the sheepfold. "Verily, verily, I say unto you, He that entereth not by the door into the sheepfold, but climbeth up some other way, the same is a thief and a robber." Here the reference is to the fold of the dry season, such as those I have already mentioned. The winter sheepfold is a roofed stone hovel called *merah*. It has one low door and no windows; therefore, by climbing up the fold, "some other way" the robber could secure no booty. The roofless fold is called *hedherah* and is built of rough stones (such as are used in New England stone fences) to the height of five feet. Above the stone construction rises a high *seyaj* (hedge) of thorny branches, securely fastened between the stones. It is this hedge which is especially designed to prevent the "thief and robber" from climbing into the sheepfold.

"But he that entereth in by the door is the shepherd of the sheep. To him the porter openeth; and the sheep hear his voice: and he calleth his own sheep by name, and leadeth them out." The shepherd's rude tent is located near the door. There also his faithful dog lies. The word "porter" in the text refers more, perhaps, to a Greek than Syrian custom. However, in case of large flocks, the under-shepherd, or the "helper," who guards the door, answers to the "porter."

The calling of the sheep or goats by name should not be taken literally. The animals are not named as persons are. The shepherd *knows* all the members of his flock by certain individual characteristics, and realizes the fact quickly when one of them is lost. The more prominent ones are given adjectival names, such as the "pure white," the "striped," the "black," the "brown," the "gray-eared," etc. But it should be borne in mind that the saying, "And he calleth his own sheep by name, and leadeth them out," indicates the tender love of the shepherd for his flock, but not that the animals answer to their names. They are never trained to do that. He "leadeth them out," not by calling their names, but by giving certain sounds which they recognize.

"And when he putteth forth his own sheep, he goeth before them, and the sheep follow him: for they know his voice." I find that the strong emphasis which commentators in general place upon the shepherd's going *before* the flock carries the impression that he does so *invariably*. So far as I know, this is not absolutely correct. *As a rule*, the shepherd goes before the flock, but not infrequently he is seen behind it. The shepherd walks behind, especially in the evening when the flock is on its way to the fold, in order that he may gather the stragglers and protect them from the stealthy wolf. The shepherd often walks by the side of the flock, at about the middle of the line. In case of large flocks the shepherd goes before, and the helper behind.

One of the great delights of my boyhood days was the sight of the "return-ing flock" every evening on the pebbly road on the side of the hill close by our house. I go up on the housetop at dusk. As soon as I hear the swishing roar of the multitude of little sharp hoofs on the stony road, which is like the sound of an approaching hailstorm among the trees, then I know that the "blessed ones" are near. The long line of horny and hornless heads sweeps down the slope of the hill like an army on a "double-quick." With his strong, protecting staff in hand, the stalwart, tender, ever-watchful shepherd ap-pears at the end of the line, and like an overshadowing Providence *guides* his beloved flock safely over the little stream and into the fold.

The effective, and, I might say, unerring, guidance of the shepherd is espe-cially shown when he leads his flock in the "narrow paths." In Syria as a rule the fields are not fenced. The pastures and the planted fields are separated by narrow footpaths, and here and there by low stone walls, which are in-tended, however, more for landmarks than for fences. The fields are the for-bidden ground. In transferring his flock from one pasture to another, the shepherd must not allow any of his animals to stray from the beaten path into the fields. For if he does, he will not only have to pay damages to the owners of the fields, but will ruin his own reputation as a shepherd. In my home town we had a shepherd who was widely famed for his skill in leading his flock in the narrow paths. Sa'ied, who supplied our community with goat's milk during the summer, was often known to guide a flock of about one hundred and fifty head of goats (which are much more unruly than sheep) without a helper, in a narrow path or over a stone wall, for a consid-erable distance, without allowing a single one of them to set foot on the for-bidden ground. The flock obeyed him because they *knew his voice* as that of their good shepherd.

It was no doubt such shepherds as Sa'ied that lent the writer of the twenty-third Psalm his telling figure. It was the faithful guidance of such earthly shepherds that led the ancient singer to meditate upon the Lord's faithful-ness to his own, and to utter his faith in the line, "He leadeth me in the paths of righteousness for his name's sake." The fields of temptation lie on either side of the narrow path of rectitude and life. The Lord will protect and lead in the right path all those who know Him and hear His voice.

Another enchanting picture of Syrian pastoral life is the gathering of the flock. The shepherd seeks and gathers his sheep for the purpose of transfer-ring them to a richer pasture, or, at the end of the day, to lead them back to the fold. He stands in the midst of the far-scattered flock and gives certain sounds, which are to the sheep what the notes of a bugle are to an army. His trained right arm, whose long range and precision are proverbial, sends the pebbles whirring in all directions, and thus "turns back" the more heedless of the flock. It was this which the Psalmist had in mind when he said, "He re-storeth my soul." The Arabic phrase *yeriddo nefsee*, means, "he turns back my soul," and refers to the action of the shepherd in turning the course of his sheep toward himself. The faithful shepherd never proceeds to lead his flock away until he is assured that all his dumb companions are gathered together.

With what pathos does the prophet Ezekiel portray this pastoral scene when he speaks of the infinite compassion of the divine shepherd of Israel, who never slumbers nor sleeps! In the thirty-fourth chapter, the eleventh verse, the promise to scattered Israel is, "For thus saith the Lord God: Behold, I, even I, will both search for my sheep, and seek them out. As a shepherd seeketh out his flock in the day that he is among his sheep that are scattered; so will I seek out my sheep, and will deliver them out of all the places where they have been scattered in the cloudy and dark day. And I will bring them out from the people, and gather them from the countries, and will bring them to their own land, and feed them upon the mountains of Israel by the rivers, and in all the inhabited places of the country. I will feed them in a good pasture, and upon the high mountains of Israel shall their fold be; there shall they lie in a good fold, and in a fat pasture shall they feed upon the mountains of Israel.... I will seek that which was lost, and bring again that which was driven away."

The climax of the shepherd figure, as it is used in the tenth chapter of the Gospel of John, is reached in Christ's saying, "I am the good shepherd: the good shepherd giveth his life for the sheep," and in the twenty-third Psalm, in the passage, "Though I walk through the valley of the shadow of death, I will fear no evil; for thou art with me: thy rod and thy staff, they comfort me." Only those who have heard the howling of a faithful shepherd at the approach of a wild beast to the flock can clearly realize how literally true is this saying of Christ's: "The good shepherd giveth his life for the sheep."

Of all the shepherds I have known or have known about in my native land, the commanding figure of one—Yusuf Balua'—rises most prominently before me. I never want to forget old Yusuf. He was over sixty when I first knew him. He was every inch a shepherd, having known no other vocation in all his life. I knew that elemental man in the "lowlands," where I spent two winters with my father, who was called thither to erect several farmhouses for the lord of the land. Yusuf, as he himself expressed it, "revered" my father; therefore, I was always welcome to visit Yusuf at his cave in the rocky gorge, and to roam with him and his flock whenever my duties as my father's helper permitted.

The flocks are kept in the "lowlands" until after the "time of birth," which comes in March; then they are led up into the mountains. It was during that blessed time of birth, and while with Yusuf, that I first beheld the original of that infinitely tender picture which is drawn in the fortieth chapter of Isaiah, the eleventh verse, and which is also Christ's most appealing picture. "He shall feed his flock like a shepherd," says the prophet; "he shall gather the lambs with his arm, and carry them in his bosom, and shall gently lead those that are with young." The text is very effectively improved by the marginal note which says, "and shall gently lead those that *give suck*." It was that which Yusuf Balua' was doing once when I happened to be with him. His

100

roughly hewn figure stands now before me, with three newly born lambs held close to his bosom, and their wilted heads resting on his massive arm. He walked gently before the anxious, slowly moving mothers, which came close behind him, emitting low, humming sounds, through which Nature poured out her compassionate heart.

"Let me carry one of them," I begged Yusuf. "No, my boy, not the helpless ones," answered the tender friend. "They need the shepherd's care now. Besides, the mothers don't know you and they would fear." But they knew *his* voice and followed him!

Oh, if we will but know and trust and follow our heavenly Shepherd, as the sheep trust and follow theirs!

But I must not lose sight of what I have called the climax of the shepherd figure in the Gospel and the Psalms; namely, the shepherd's interposing with his own life between the flock and the wolf. The wolf, the hyena, and the leopard are the flock's most formidable foes. During his long life Yusuf fought many battles with those ferocious beasts, but never lost a hoof to them in all those encounters. On more than one occasion he followed the hyena to his lair, and, by his characteristic howling, flinging his deadly stones with his sling, and striking with his heavy staff on the rocks, compelled the beast to abandon his prey. Whether the unfortunate sheep was yet alive or whether it had died, Yusuf, as a good and faithful shepherd, always carried it back to the fold. Does not the prophet Amos assure Israel of their Shepherd's infinite care for them in an allusion to the faithful seeking by the earthly shepherd for even a fragment of his lost sheep? "Thus saith Jehovah," cries Amos; "As the shepherd *rescueth out of the mouth of the lion two legs, or a piece of an ear*; so shall the children of Israel be rescued." [1] To this care and devotion of the shepherd, Jesus also alludes in his parabolic saying in which he speaks of his having "come to save that which was lost." "How think ye? if a man have an hundred sheep, and one of them be gone astray, doth he not leave the ninety and nine, and goeth into the mountains, and seeketh that which is gone astray? And if so be that he find it, verily I say unto you, he rejoiceth more of that sheep, than of the ninety and nine which went not astray. Even so it is not the will of your Father which is in heaven, that one of these little ones should perish!" [2]

When I think of that deep, rocky gorge where Yusuf wintered with his flock, and the many similar valleys which the Syrian shepherds have to traverse daily; when I think of the wild beasts they have to fight, of the scars they bear on their bodies as marks of their unreserved and boundless devotion to their flocks, I realize very clearly the depth of the Psalmist's faith when he said, "Though I walk through the valley of the shadow of death, I will fear no evil; for thou art with me: thy rod and thy staff, they comfort me."

[1] Amos iii: 12. Revised Version.   [2] Matt. xviii: 12-14.

Part Five - Sisters of Mary and Martha

Chapter One - Woman East and West

Perhaps on no other subject do the Orient and the Occident diverge more widely than on that of the status of woman. So far as they really differ, and as they imagine that they differ in their regard for woman, the Orientals and the Occidentals form two distinct human types.

From the beginning of their history, the Teutonic races, especially the Anglo-Saxons, have been characterized by their high regard for woman. This trait of the dwellers of north-western Europe so impressed the Latin Christian missionaries, when they first visited those peoples, that they described them as having "such high regard for woman to the extent that adultery was unknown among them." And while the concluding phrase of this historical testimony does not describe the present state of Anglo-Saxon society with absolute correctness, the statement as a whole seems to me to be a substantially correct description of present Anglo-Saxon life. Among the peoples of north-western Europe, and especially among their descendants in America, woman enjoys man's highest regard.

On the other hand, "the Oriental view of woman" has always been considered by those Western peoples to be very contemptuous. We always hate most deeply that vice which is the opposite of our strongest virtue. We are most likely to exaggerate and to condemn mercilessly any deviation from that which we ourselves consider to be the sacred path of duty. Respect for woman being one of his strongest virtues, the Anglo-Saxon is lashed to fury by what seems to him to be the Oriental's utter disrespect for the mother of the race.

As I have already stated in other connections in this work, my object is neither to accuse the Oriental nor to excuse his moral failures. My aim is rather to interpret him to my Western readers and to determine, if possible, to what extent he really is a transgressor of the normal rules of behavior toward woman. My intimate knowledge of life in both hemispheres and my affectionate regard for the good qualities of both the Orientals and the Occidentals lead me to venture to be a reconciler of their differences. They certainly misunderstand one another, especially with reference to the domestic and social relations of the sexes. Time was when the various races hugged their prejudices close to their own hearts and really enjoyed ridiculing one another.

But "the hour cometh and now is" when the peoples of the earth are beginning to realize that righteousness and truth, kindness and good manners, are the exclusive possessions of no one race. The peoples of the earth are beginning to realize that a mutual sympathetic understanding between the various races is an asset of civilization, and a promoter of the cause of that human commonwealth for which all good men pray and hope. Therefore, as one who owes much to both the East and the West, I deem it my duty to do what I can to promote such a sympathetic understanding, without doing violence to the truth.

What is an obvious fact, and which can by no means be ignored, even by the most zealous special pleader, is that the Eastern woman is far from being the equal of her Western sister, either in culture or in domestic and social privileges. Perhaps in no other country does woman enjoy these blessings to the extent to which the American woman enjoys them. Woman as man's intellectual companion, as a promoter of ideals, as a factor in domestic and social evolution, the Orient has never known. The Western type of woman is now partially represented in my native land by a minority of cultivated women, but their number is comparatively very small.

The Oriental social code (if the simple social usages in that part of the world may be termed such) gives man the precedence. To give woman the social and domestic prominence, the little attentions and courtesies which she enjoys in America, is to the Orientals not only unnecessary, but uncomplimentary to both sexes.

It is perhaps for lack of such attentions and courtesies, more than for anything else, that the Occidentals consider the Oriental woman to be the slave of her husband. And, conversely, because of his giving the precedence to woman in all the courtesies and comforts of life, the Orientals, *both men and women*, consider the Occidental to be the slave of his wife. How often have I heard Syrians say, "An *affrenjee* [that is, a European] is quite a man until his wife whispers something to him. Then he becomes her slave; he does just what she tells him."

The Oriental's indifference to those fine points of behavior toward woman does not spring from the fact that he considers her to be intrinsically his inferior, and consequently his slave. I never had the slightest reason, nor the faintest suggestion, either by example or precept, to believe that my mother was in any way my father's inferior. "Thou shalt honour thy father *and* thy mother" is a commandment which was born of the deepest life of the East. I can think of no circumstances in Eastern life which compel a Syrian to think of his mother, sister, and wife in other than terms of equality in all essentials with the male members of the family. [1]

In my judgment it is the Oriental's deportment, rather than his real intentions, which condemns him in the sight of Occidentals for his attitude toward woman. It is perhaps hazardous to undertake to differentiate between character and conduct, between the motive and the method by which that motive is put into action. It is customary, however, to say of a person that "his heart is in the right place, but he does not know how to act." I venture to say that this characterization fits the case of the average Oriental. His heart is in the right place. His natural endowments are good. He is quick-witted, kind,

103

generous, pious, obedient to parents, and a lover of his home. So far as all these fundamentals are concerned, I find no great difference between the Easterners and the Westerners.

However, compared with his Western cousin, the son of the Near East has only a slight acquaintance with the *art* of living. The working-out of details with the view of creating harmony has always seemed to him vanity and vexation of spirit. His intense desire for simple, spontaneous, easy living has always refused to be encumbered by exacting standards. In this respect he is a boy in man's clothing. For an example, the home to him is little more than a shelter. The riches of the home are not the artistic appointments, but human associations. Architectural schemes, interior decorations, books, musical instruments, living by the clock, and other Western glories are to the Oriental dispensable luxuries. The one-room or two-room house, very simply furnished, is the essential part of the home. Why then should one be burdened with more? The "color scheme," the harmony or contrast of wall-paper with picture frames and carpets, and the thousand and one articles of useful and ornamental furniture which crowd the American home and make the "servant-girl problem" well-nigh insoluble, are to the average Oriental a delusion and a snare. His table appointments are also very simple. To him the "one thing needful" is enough food to sustain life. He has no "cook-book." The varieties of cake and pie, and the multitude of side dishes which load the American table, do not appear on the Syrian's bill of fare. One dish of cooked cereals, or meat and rice or some other wholesome combination, and a few loaves of bread, satisfy his hunger. His modest stores of grape molasses, figs, and raisins, which he visits at irregular intervals, satisfy his craving for sweets, and his home-made wine gives color and gayety to his feasts.

The same simple rules govern the Oriental's social activities. Whether as an individual or as a domestic and social being, he hates to be standardized. To him formalities have no claim upon those who are true friends and social equals. Spontaneous living must not be too closely yoked with etiquette, nor native wisdom with technical culture. "*Meta weck'at elmahabbet artafa' ettekleef*" (when love occurs formalities cease) is one of the Oriental's ancient and cherished maxims. From early childhood the Americans are taught to observe, even within the family circle, the niceties of "Please," "Thank you," "Pardon me," "I beg your pardon," "May I trouble you," and so forth. To a son of the East such behavior is altogether proper among strangers, but not among those who really *love one another*. Between husband and wife, parent and child, brothers and sisters, and true friends such formalities appear to Easterners not only superficial, but utterly ridiculous. For such persons the most essential thing is that they should love one another. As lovers they have a right to *demand* favors from one another. The commands of love are sweet; they must not be alloyed with tiresome formalities.

Of course this "friendliness" of the Oriental is not altogether an unmixed blessing. He relies too much upon his good intentions, which his conduct does not always show. Judged, not only by Western standards, but by the

104

standards of the cultivated minority of his own people, he is found wanting. It is not always easy for him to be familiar without being vulgar, and to distinguish between the legitimate claims of friendship and intrusion upon the exclusive rights of others. His plea always is that he means well, which is generally true. "His heart is in the right place."

Now I believe it can be easily seen that the Easterner's attitude toward woman, which now rises to the height of religious reverence, now verges on contempt, is to be traced to his uneven, juvenile temperament and lack of culture, and not to the fact that he despises her. So long as he respects her "in his heart" and is ready to defend her at whatever cost, he considers the fine points of conduct toward her after the American fashion to be simply dispensable little details. Nor does his attitude toward woman differ essentially from his attitude toward the male portion of mankind. He has one vocabulary for both sexes, with the inclination to be more respectful toward the gentler sex.

So woman in the East is not considered a slave by the man, and there is a multitude of wife-ruled husbands. The family system, however, is patriarchal. The man is recognized as the "lord of the household." The venerable father of a family is supposed to rule, not only over the women of the household, but over his grown sons, his younger brothers, and even the men of his clan who are younger than himself. But such an authority is often purely formal. The higher the level of culture in the home, the more freedom and equality exists among the members of the family. In cultivated Syrian homes the women are free and highly and uniformly respected by the men. Such women have no reason to envy even the happiest American women.

[1] My statements apply particularly to the Christian women of Syria, who enjoy greater domestic and social privileges than the Mohammedan women. However, notwithstanding the serious limitations which orthodox Mohammedanism imposes upon women, it would be sheer injustice to the better class of Mohammedans to be stigmatized as enslavers and debasers of woman.

Chapter Two - Paul and Woman

Perhaps nowhere else is the Syrian attitude toward woman so clearly stated as in the teachings of St. Paul. The great Apostle deals with the fundamentals of this subject, and speaks freely of both the privileges and the limitations of woman in the Christian East.

In the third chapter of the Epistle to the Galatians, the twenty-eighth verse, Paul says, "There is neither male nor female: for ye are all one in Christ Jesus." And this equality is not to be understood to be limited to the bestowal of church rites upon men and women alike. It embraces the essential points of conduct of the male and female members of the household toward one another. Fidelity to the marriage vow is to be equally observed by both husband and wife. This the Apostle urges upon his fellow believers, not as a superior authority, but as a friend. In the seventh chapter of the First Epistle to the Corinthians, the fourth verse, he says, "The wife hath not power over her own body, but the husband; and *likewise* also the husband hath not power over his own body, but the wife." In the fourteenth verse of this same chapter, the equal potency of the spiritual influence of both the husband and the wife is also recognized. "The unbelieving husband," says the Apostle, "is sanctified by the wife, and the unbelieving wife is sanctified by the husband." In the fifth chapter of the Epistle to the Ephesians, the "Apostle to the Gentiles" rises to the noblest height of Eastern thought concerning woman and reveals Christianity's conserving and sanctifying power. Beginning at the twenty-fifth verse, he says: "Husbands, love your wives, even as Christ also loved the church, and gave himself for it; that he might sanctify and cleanse it, ... that he might present it to himself a glorious church, not having spot, or wrinkle, or any such thing; but that it should be holy and without blemish. So ought men to love their wives as their own bodies. He that loveth his wife loveth himself. For no man ever yet hated his own flesh; but nourisheth and cherisheth it, even as the Lord the church."

This is precisely what the marriage union in the East always meant to us. By this sacred bond the husband and the wife are made "one flesh." That the Oriental has not definitely succeeded in making his daily conduct always conform to his highest ideals and to the noble precepts of the Gospel is evident, and not at all strange. Here he has succeeded no better than his Anglo-Saxon superior has in conforming his conduct to the command, "Love your enemies." My point is that down deep in the Syrian heart the spirit of Paul's words abides. It serves the son of the East in time of trouble as his quick and tender conscience. The real trouble with him has been his aversion to strictly systematic living. He does love his wife as he loves himself, but in reality he does not fully know how to love himself.

Paul, on the other hand, does not ignore the conventional limitations which Eastern traditions impose upon woman. He recognizes the patriarchal government of the family. In the chapter just quoted, the Apostle says: "Wives, submit yourselves unto your own husbands, as unto the Lord. For the husband is the head of the wife, even as Christ is the head of the Church." Much trouble may be avoided by the unfriendly critics of Paul and Christianity in general, if such critics would keep in mind the conditional nature of this command. Whether as a Syrian or as an American I do not believe in subjecting the wife to the husband, nor the husband to the wife. Domestic life should be based on perfect coöperation of husband and wife, in spiritual as well as in administrative matters. Toward this goal the Americans have made the greatest advance. However, Paul's command can by no means be justly construed as giving the husband unlimited tyrannical authority over the wife. "The husband is the head of the wife, *even as Christ is the head of the Church.*" The church is not the slave of Christ, but his beloved bride. So the supremacy here is that of loving care and consideration. Therefore, the fact that the traditions of the East give the man conventional supremacy over the woman has never meant to us sons of that land that our mothers and sisters were abject slaves. And it should be borne in mind that the women of Syria are not always so submissive as those traditions would lead a Westerner to believe. I might say that in the majority of cases the man finds it no easy task to make his formal authority over the woman of real effect. The heartfelt complaints of discouraged husbands, that "not even all the angels of heaven can subdue a woman," are not unfrequently heard in the land of the Bible.

Perhaps the part of Paul's teaching which seems to Westerners to seal the fate of woman is that found in the eleventh chapter of the First Epistle to the Corinthians. Here the Apostle declares: "For a man indeed ought not to cover his head, forasmuch as he is the image and glory of God: but the woman is the glory of the man. Neither was the man created for the woman; but the woman for the man."

I think any serious Bible student will easily realize that as a good shepherd Paul must have felt that he should not travel much faster than the weakest of his flock. In the passage just quoted he stoops low for the purpose of accommodating the prejudices of *certain* Orientals. And in so doing he contradicts his own saying, "There is neither male nor female: for ye are all one in Christ Jesus," and the great passage in the first chapter of Genesis, the twenty-seventh verse, "So God created man in his own image, in the image of God created he him; *male and female* created he them."

The Eastern man has from time immemorial decreed that woman's social privileges should be limited, because of his fear for her. In such an unstable social order as that which has existed in the East for ages woman is constantly exposed to danger. Woman-stealing was very prevalent in ancient times, and is still practiced among the Arabian tribes which hover on the eastern borders of Syria. In modern Syria such practices no longer exist, but their faint echoes are still heard in times of tribal fights. On such occasions the cry is heard (and I often heard it myself), "You dogs, to-day we shall take your women booty [*nesbee hereemekûm*]."

It is because of these ancient fears, and not from a desire on the part of the man to enslave her, that the social privileges of the woman in the East are so limited. The duty to protect always carries with it the right to discipline. And the greater the danger, the more strict the discipline. The weaker men of the clan, because they need to be protected, are also in subjection to the "men of counsel" (*ahil erry*) and to the stronger fighters.

And it may be easily inferred that in such circumstances woman's charms are a danger to her. She must be secluded, as among the Mohammedans, or simply limited in her social intercourse, as among the Christians, in order to hide those charms from the curious stranger. For this reason also she must be heavily veiled when she goes out, as among the Moslems, or at least have her head covered always, as among the Christians. So when Paul said, "Every woman that prayeth or prophesieth with her head uncovered dishonoreth her head," [1] he simply gave wise recognition to an ancient social custom. A more liberal course on his part would have marked Paul as a violent disturber of venerable traditions.

The chief charm of an Oriental woman is her *hishmat* (modesty). But modesty in a stricter sense than that accepted in the Occident. Feminine timidity (*jubn*) is very extensively sung by the Arabian poets. A charming woman, especially a maiden, is she who is timid, shy, retiring, of a few words. "She has a mouth to eat, but not to speak," is a high tribute paid to a maiden. For a woman to take a leading part in conversation in the presence of men is boldness. I do not know how they manage to do it, but, *as a rule*, in the presence of men the women of Syria exercise marvelous control over their organs of speech.

Do you understand now why Paul says, in the fourteenth chapter of his First Epistle to the Corinthians, the thirty-fourth verse, "Let your women keep silence in the Churches: for it is not permitted unto them to speak; but they are commanded to be under obedience"? To Oriental ears, as perhaps to Puritan ears of the good old type, such words are poetry set to music. They do not degrade, but honor woman by not making her common.

It would, perhaps, throw further light on the Easterners' regard of woman as a sacred being when it is known why they call the wife *hûrmat*. This term is derived from *heram*—a consecrated and wholly sacred object. *Heram* is the name of the Mohammedans' most sacred shrine of Mecca. The wife is the husband's most sacred possession, therefore she is called *hûrmat*. The plural of this is *harem*, a term which to Westerners has a most obnoxious connotation. But not so to Orientals. In the West *harem* simply means sensuality and polygamy in their worst form. In the East it means simply and purely the women of a household, or of a clan, whether it be Christian or Mohammedan. It does not necessarily mean plurality of wives. A man's mother, wife, sisters, and daughters constitute his *harem*; for they are all sacred to him.

Now it will not be difficult to understand, I believe, why it is that the man in the East takes precedence of the woman in all social affairs, and why the sexes are segregated at public feasts and on other similar occasions. It is for the same reason that we find no women disciples at the Last Supper. In the parable of the prodigal son, the father meets the returning penitent, the father bestows "the best robe" on the son, the father orders the feast, and doubtless presides over it. So it was also when Abraham entertained the angels, and Zacchæus entertained Jesus—the man was the entertainer. However, in these two cases the women might have acted as hostesses,—because the guests were holy persons. We have a striking example of the freedom which is permitted to women in such cases in the story of Mary and Martha. They entertained Jesus, first because apparently they had no parents living, and their brother was young, and second because Jesus was no mere guest, but a holy person.

Notwithstanding all these social conventions, however, the mother has a right to demand from her children the same loving obedience which they accord to their father. They must honor their father and their mother alike. Upon coming home from a journey I always saluted my parents by kissing their hands, as a mark of loving submission. According to custom, I saluted my father first, and my mother second, but in the same identical manner, and invoked their *radha* (good pleasure) toward me, with religious reverence. I always knew that to disrespect and disobey my mother was not only bad manners, but a sin. So obnoxious has disobedience to parents been to the respectable families of the East that the ancient Israelites made it a capital crime. In the twenty-first chapter of the Book of Deuteronomy the stipulation of the law is: "If a man have a stubborn and rebellious son, which will not obey the voice of his father, or the voice of *his mother*, and that, when they have chastened him, will not hearken unto them: then shall his father *and* his mother lay hold on him, and bring him out unto the elders of his city, and unto the gate of his place; and they shall say unto the elders of his city, This our son is stubborn and rebellious, he will not obey our voice.... And all the men of his city shall stone him with stones, that he die." [2] Needless to say that this cruel punishment is no longer inflicted upon rebellious sons in the East. The record, however, indicates the joint authority of the husband and wife over their own children, and the public approval of it.

But there is more to be said about *radha-elwalideen* (the parents' good pleasure). I do not know whether the words "good pleasure" convey the real significance of the word *radha*, which as it pertains to parents is one of the most sacred terms in Oriental speech. The *radha* of a parent is a benediction which includes complete forgiveness to the child of all offenses and indicates the parent's spiritual satisfaction with his offspring. To secure the parent's expressed *radha* at the hour of death is equal to a sacrament. I can think of no human experience that can be more impressive, more tender, and more deeply religious than that of an Oriental imploring a dying parent to assure him of his or her *radha* before the end came. The weeping son grasps the hand of his dying parent, and, leaning over tenderly to catch the faint utterances, says: "Father, [3] bestow your *radha* upon me; forgive me and bless me, so that Allah also may forgive and bless me; your *radha*, father!" If the departing parent is still able to speak, he looks up toward heaven and says: "You have my *radha*, my dearly beloved son; and may Allah bestow his holy *radha* upon you and bless you and the work of your hands. May the earth produce riches for you, and heaven shower benedictions upon you; pray for me, my dearly beloved." But if the departing father or mother is no longer able to utter words, the repeated pressing of the hand and the turning of the eyes upward indicate the parent's response to the petition of the son or daughter. The refusal of a parent to grant his *radha*, which is most rare, is to an Oriental a haunting horror.

In ancient Israel the deathbed blessing was bestowed with special emphasis upon the first-born son because with it came the heritage of the patriarchal office. Thus, when Isaac bestowed his last blessing upon his tricky son Jacob, he said: [4] "God give thee of the dew of heaven, and the fatness of the earth, and plenty of corn and wine: Let people serve thee, and nations bow down to thee: be lord over thy brethren, and let thy mother's sons bow down to thee." And what is also most touching in this story is poor Esau's agony when he discovered that the blessing to which he was the rightful heir had gone to his brother. "And Esau said unto his father, Hast thou but one blessing, my father? bless me, even me also, O my father. And Esau lifted up his voice and wept." [5]

[1] 1 Cor. xi: 5.
[2] Verses 18-21.
[3] The same also is asked of the mother.

[4] Gen. xxvii: 28, 29.
[5] Gen. xxvii: 38.

Chapter Three - Jesus and His Mother

One of the perplexing passages in the New Testament is that found in the fourth verse of the second chapter of St. John's Gospel, where Jesus says to his mother, "Woman, what have I to do with thee?" That it has been very difficult for many devout readers of the Bible to reconcile this passage to the Master's gentleness and goodness is very well known to me. On numerous occasions I have been asked to give my interpretation of this saying in the light of the status of woman in the East, and to state whether, in my opinion as a Syrian, Jesus could have meant to be harsh and disrespectful to his mother. Before undertaking to give my own view of this passage, I wish to present two interpretations of it which I have heard certain American preachers give. One of those preachers who was proud to call himself "a free lance" stated in my hearing that on the occasion when Jesus spoke these words "he simply lost his temper." The redeeming feature of this comment, in my opinion, is its brevity. It is short, but neither sweet nor to the point. The other interpreter (or interpreters, for I do not recall where and when I heard this), assuming that the station of woman in the East was very low, stated that by addressing his mother in a seemingly harsh manner, Jesus infringed no rule of propriety. Having already stated at considerable length the "Oriental view of woman," I deem it necessary here simply to say that the foregoing interpretation rests on a misconception of the facts.

In trying to throw some light on this passage I will say that, notwithstanding its seeming harshness in the English translation, I find no real reason to believe that in uttering it Jesus indicated that he was angry, or that he meant to be disrespectful to his mother. This somewhat impersonal form of address to a woman is very common in the East. It *might* be so spoken as to mean disrespect, but as a rule, and according to the Oriental manner of speech, it is dignified and in good taste. At present the term *hûrmat* is more extensively used in such cases in Syria. Among the nobility and the educated minority of the people the word *sitt* (lady) is employed in addressing a woman. However,

110

this impersonal form of address is employed by a man when speaking to a woman who is a stranger to him. The correct form is, "O woman," the same which Jesus used in saying to the "woman of Canaan," in the fifteenth chapter of Matthew, the twenty-eighth verse, "O woman, great is thy faith: be it unto thee even as thou wilt." In the same manner the Master assured the woman who had "a spirit of infirmity," [1] "Woman, [2] thou art loosed from thine infirmity." A superb example of this Oriental usage is found in the fourth chapter of St. John's Gospel, the twenty-first verse, in Jesus' conversation with the Samaritan woman. With solemn dignity he says to her: "Woman, believe me, the hour cometh, when ye shall neither in this mountain, nor yet at Jerusalem, worship the Father.... But the hour cometh, and now is, when the true worshippers shall worship the Father in spirit and in truth."

From the foregoing examples it may be easily seen that the form of Jesus' address to his mother could not be considered disrespectful. Therefore the difficulty which the text offers springs from the fact that it represents Jesus as speaking to his own mother as he would speak to a woman *who was a stranger to him*. Why did he do that? The answer to this question depends partially on thorough knowledge of Oriental thought and largely on acquaintance with the theology of St. John's Gospel.

As every Bible scholar knows, the purpose of this Gospel is to present Jesus to the world as the incarnation of the Logos—the Word. Here the Master is spoken of, not as the prophet of Galilee, but as the One who came down from heaven. Therefore the Son of God was by virtue of this supernatural character above all earthly connections. His mother was only human, only finite. On the occasion of his addressing her as a stranger she is represented as interfering with him as he was about to work a miracle. Such a thing, according to St. John's Gospel, was beyond her understanding. Consequently as a *divine* being speaking to a *human* being, Jesus said to his earthly mother, "Woman, what is mine and what is thine?" This is the original form. The English translation, "Woman, what have I to do with thee," is good, although the more refined attitude of the West toward woman makes the expression seem rather harsh. Stated in simplest terms the Oriental understanding of these words is, "Leave me alone." In Jesus' case the further implication of the passage is that, as Mary's vision of spiritual things was not Jesus' vision, even though he was her son in the flesh, she was not competent to exercise authority over him, seeing that he was a divine being. In a higher sense she was a stranger to him.

With real consistency the writer of the Fourth Gospel clings to this view of Jesus' divinity to the end. In the nineteenth chapter we find the Master speaking from the cross. He speaks, not as a human sufferer, but as a triumphant heavenly being. He addresses his mother in the same manner as he did at the marriage feast in Cana of Galilee—"Woman." In the twenty-fifth verse it is said: "Now there stood by the Cross of Jesus his mother, and his mother's sister, Mary the wife of Cleophas, and Mary Magdalene. When Jesus therefore saw his mother, and the disciple standing by, whom he loved, he saith unto his mother, Woman, behold thy son!" In this lofty yet tender manner the Master committed his loving mother to the care of his beloved disciple.

The excellent qualities of a man are credited by Orientals largely to *haleeb el-omm* (the mother's milk) and the mysterious influences of the prenatal period. Aside from its nutritive qualities, *el-redha'* (suck) is supposed to possess certain mystic influences which tend to fashion the possibilities of character. Whenever a man, especially a youth, speaks "words of wisdom," his admiring hearer is likely to exclaim, "Precious was the milk that nourished thee!" Among the choice blessings which Jacob asked for Joseph the patriarch did not forget to include the "blessings of the breasts, and of the womb." [3] Nothing can be loftier to an Oriental than the passage in the eleventh chapter of St. Luke's gospel, the twenty-seventh verse. Jesus is represented in the preceding verses as disputing triumphantly with his theological adversaries. His trenchant periods, "Every kingdom divided against itself is brought to desolation.... He that is not with me is against me," and his simple yet profound reasoning that a human heart which is not filled with the spirit of God is bound to become the abode of evil spirits, deeply stir his hearers. So the text tells us, "A certain woman of the company lifted up her voice and said unto him, Blessed is the womb that bare thee, and the breasts which thou hast sucked!"

The most solemn occasion on which I heard this expression used in my native land was that when the great Patriarch of Antioch visited our town in Mount Lebanon. Upon his arrival at the priest's house, where he was entertained, the waiting multitude, including the governor of the district, stood with bowed heads to receive the prelate's benediction. I shall never forget that scene. Standing in the door, our revered and beloved patriarch seemed to us to be a visitor from the celestial sphere, full of truth and grace. As he lifted his right arm and imparted his blessing to the silent assemblage, a woman of our church, a mother, who was almost overcome with emotion, advanced toward the spiritual ruler, and with her face and open palms turned toward heaven, exclaimed, in the vernacular Arabic, "Blessed be the inwards that bore you, and the breasts you sucked!" Whereupon the distinguished visitor bestowed a special blessing upon the humble suppliant, to the great satisfaction of the profoundly affected multitude.

[1] Luke xiii: 12.

[2] The English translation changes the form, "O woman" to "Woman" arbitrarily.

[3] Gen. xlix: 25.

Chapter Four - "A Gracious Woman"

To the East woman is known only as wife and mother, and, of course, as the home-maker. The statement, "Woman's place is in the home," is never a matter of dispute in that part of the world. In the home are to be found both "woman's rights" and woman's duties. Education, literary pursuits, "club life," and civic endeavors are no vital interests to the Eastern woman, nor to her husband to any appreciable extent. Marriage is a religious union. The highest and most sacred duty of the husband and wife is to beget many children, bring them up "in the fear of the Lord," and be such good example to them, as to enable them to live a pious life, and to transmit their good heritage to the unborn generations. Marriage of inclination, preceded by a period of courtship as in the West, is very rare in the East. The reason of this has been hinted in the preceding chapters. Lack of education and social and political stability necessitates the curtailing of woman's social privileges, for her own safety. These limitations are especially narrow in the case of "maidens," or "virgins"; that is, unmarried young women. They are not supposed to participate in social functions as their mothers do, nor to form friendships with young men, even among their near relatives. The contracting of a marriage is not so much an individual as it is a clannish affair. The young people may, or may not be acquainted with one another. Among Christians, the young man may frequent the home of his future wife's parents, and even converse with her now and then, but only in the presence of other members of the family. "Going with a young lady" is unknown to the East, and is a feature of Western life which Orientals generally condemn. The marriage is agreed upon by the families or clans of the contracting parties, because the family or clan is involved in the conduct and affected by the reputation of each one of its members. The shame of a woman is a burden to all her kindred. Interclannish marriages form alliances and impose defensive and offensive obligations. Whenever a woman of one clan, who is married into another, is cruelly treated by her husband, her own clansmen are supposed to rise and defend her, else they become a byword in the community.

This difference of procedure between the East and the West in contracting a marriage does not seem to result in a decidedly marked difference in domestic happiness. In both the East and the West, the perfectly happy and the perfectly unhappy marriages are rare. In both hemispheres the large majority of married people soon learn that domestic happiness depends in no small measure on adherence to the well-known rule: "In essentials unity; in nonessentials liberty; in all things charity." As I have already stated, the Oriental does not know the art of living as the Occidental does, yet the Easterner enjoys as much home happiness as those Occidentals who are on the same level of culture with him.

Women in the East are classified, not with reference to education and social interests or the lack of them, but with reference to virtue and its opposite. A happy husband says, "I lift my head high [arfa' rasy] because of my wife. Her siett [reputation] is like musk in fragrance. She is taj rasy [a crown to my head]." So also speaks the writer of the Book of Proverbs, in the twelfth chapter, and the fourth verse: "A virtuous woman is a crown to her husband: but she that maketh ashamed is as rottenness in his bones." In both the East and the West the opinion is accepted that "as a jewel of gold in a swine's snout, so is a fair woman which is without discretion." [1]

The Orient and the Occident diverge considerably in their description of feminine charms in poetry and literature. Here I find the Orientals to be very inconsistent. Their strong aversion to the free mention of women in conversation and to her sharing of social privileges equally with the man, contrasts very sharply with their license in describing her charms in their poetry. A most perfect specimen of this poetry in the Bible is Solomon's Song. Its Oriental freedom in describing the "beloved spouse," renders it practically unfit for public use. Its poetical charms are exquisite, and its passion is pure, but judged by Western standards, the faithfulness of its realism appears licentious. It is exhilarating to read the poet's lines in which he calls his "fair one" to go with him into the fields and vineyards.

> "Rise up, my love, my fair one, and come away.
> For, lo, the winter is past,
> The rain is over and gone;
> The flowers appear on the earth;
> The time of the singing of birds is come,
> And the voice of the turtle dove is heard in our land;
> The fig tree ripeneth her green figs,
> And the vines are in blossom,
> They give forth their fragrance.
> Arise, my love, my fair one, and come away.
> O my dove, that art in the clefts of the rock,
> In the covert of the steep place,
> Let me see thy countenance,
> Let me hear thy voice;
> For sweet is thy voice, and thy countenance is comely." [2]

In the opening verses of the fourth chapter the poet's vision of his "love" is also beautiful.

> "Behold, thou art fair, my love; behold, thou art fair;
> Thine eyes are as doves behind thy veil:
> Thy hair is as a flock of goats,
> That lie along the side of mount Gilead.
> Thy teeth are like a flock of ewes that are newly shorn
> Which are come up from the washing; ...
> Thy lips are like a thread of scarlet,
> And thy mouth is comely."

All this is beautiful and perfectly acceptable to both the East and the West. Not so the opening lines of the seventh chapter. The Revised Version modifies the original text. King James's Version gives the lines just as Oriental poetry past and present would render them. The rendering of the second verse by the Revised Version, "Thy body is like a round goblet," and, "Thy waist is like an heap of wheat," renders the words meaningless. However, the modesty of the revisers is to be commended.

Arabic poetry is full of such passages, which abound also in Syrian vernacular songs, which are sung with perfect propriety among all classes. In discussing such a subject as this one can hardly resist the temptation to judge. To me the more chaste way of the West in poetizing feminine charms is far superior to the altogether too free realism of the East, which I do not feel at all inclined to defend. Yet I would not be loyal to good conscience if I did not offer an explanation in behalf of the land of my birth. Ever since I began to read Arabic poetry, for which I developed great fondness, to the present day, I do not remember that its descriptions of feminine loveliness ever really suggested to me licentious thoughts. The general effect of such delineations upon me was of the same sort as that which the sketching of love scenes by a great novelist produces. Its charms were those of the poetic art, and not those of the seductive feelings of sordid passion.

To us 'aroos esshi'ar (the bride, or spouse of the poet) is purely an imaginary creature. It is the poet's spirit of inspiration objectified in a female form. He does not describe a woman, but an angelic creature whose body and soul are both pure. Only the very commonplace versifier gets demoralized and infects his reader with the same feeling. The true poet soars far above "the things that perish," and is perfectly safe to follow. His infatuation is known as el howa el'adhry (pure, or aspirational love). Here, then, without the slightest attempt to excuse his phraseology, I find at least a partial justification for the Eastern poet, and for the writer of Solomon's Song.

The simple, eloquent, and fully inclusive description of the "virtuous woman," in the thirty-first chapter of the Book of Proverbs, is rather a composite than an individual picture. It expresses the Syrian's noblest idea of the true wife and the real home-maker:—

Who can find a virtuous woman? for her price is far above rubies.

The heart of her husband doth safely trust in her, so that he shall have no need for spoil.

She will do him good and not evil all the days of her life.

She seeketh wool, and flax, and worketh willingly with her hands.

She is like the merchant's ships; she bringeth her food from afar.

She riseth also while it is yet night, and giveth meat to her household, and a portion to her maidens.

She considereth a field, and buyeth it: with the fruits of her hands she planteth a vineyard.

She girdeth her loins with strength, and strengtheneth her arms.

She perceiveth that her merchandise is good: her candle goeth not out by night.

She layeth her hands to the spindle, and her hands hold the distaff.

She stretcheth out her hands to the poor; yea, she reacheth forth her hands to the needy.

She is not afraid of the snow for her household: for all her household are clothed with scarlet.

She maketh herself coverings of tapestry; her clothing is silk and purple.

Her husband is known in the gates, when he sitteth among the elders of the land.

She maketh fine linen, and selleth it; and delivereth girdles unto the merchant.

Strength and honor are her clothing; and she shall rejoice in time to come.

She openeth her mouth with wisdom; and in her tongue is the law of kindness.

She looketh well to the ways of her household, and eateth not the bread of idleness.

Her children arise up, and call her blessed; her husband also, and he praiseth her.

Many daughters have done virtuously, but thou excellest them all.

Favour is deceitful, and beauty is vain: but a woman that feareth the Lord, she shall be praised.

Give her of the fruit of her hands; and let her own works praise her in the gates.

Here we have the real "Oriental view of woman," and a glorification of virtue, loyalty, industry, wisdom, kindness, and charity, unsurpassed in its beauty and simplicity. I have said that this remarkable picture is rather composite than individual. Yet the true, diligent, and virtuous Syrian wife and mother comes near being the ideal woman of the ancient Scriptural writer. His question, "Who can find a virtuous woman?" does not mean that such a woman cannot be found; nor his saying, "For her price is far above rubies" mean that women are bought and sold in the market. The sense of the writer can be adequately expressed by saying, "Happy is he who hath a virtuous woman, for her worth is far above all earthly riches." But for the existence of women approaching his ideal, this writer could not have given the world his picture of the "virtuous woman."

I feel that no detailed commentary on these verses is needed. The virtues here enumerated are universally cherished. I will, however, call attention to the Oriental features of this great passage. In saying that "the heart of her husband doth safely trust in her," the writer shows that the good wife is by no means a despised creature in the Syrian home. She is loved and trusted as her husband's life-partner, and exerts no inconsiderable influence upon him. The value of such a wife's counsel in the estimation of her husband and friends is also indicated in the saying, "She openeth her mouth with wisdom; and in her tongue is the law of kindness." "She seeketh wool, and flax, and worketh willingly with her hands," or, as the Arabic version has it, "with willing hands." The flax is now rarely found in Syria. Wool and silk cocoons are spun into thread by means of the spindle, woven on hand looms, and made into garments by the women, especially in the rural districts. This verse should be joined to verse nineteen, which says, "She layeth her hands to the spindle, and her hands hold the distaff." The Revised Version says, "She layeth her hands to the distaff, and her hands hold the spindle." In explaining this passage some commentators speak of the spinning wheel, and of the distaff, as the dictionary defines it: "A rotating vertical staff that holds the bunch of flax or wool in hand-spinning." But this is not the "spindle" which is intended in the passage before us. The Syrian spindle (*meghzel*) which a woman may carry wherever she goes, is a small instrument. It consists of a smooth wooden pin, or stem, about the size and shape of a long wooden pen holder. This is inserted at its thick end into a hole of a hemispherical "top" or whorl, which is the exact shape of the crown of a small mushroom. It is this top which the English translation calls "distaff." A small brass hook fastened to the end of the stem, which protrudes slightly above the whorl, completes the spindle. In spinning a quantity of wool is wound on a small wooden or wire frame into which the woman inserts her left hand, the frame passing over the fingers and held inside the palm next to the thumb, thus leaving the thumb and all the fingers free. The spinner fastens the hook of the spindle to the bunch of wool and twirls the spindle swiftly at its lower end, between the thumb and the middle finger of the right hand, and then draws the thread deftly with the fingers of both hands. When the twisted thread is about the "length of an arm," the spinner unhooks it without breaking it off, winds it on the stem of the spindle, just below the whorl, then fastens it again to the hook close to the raw material. The operation is thus continued until the bunch of wool is converted into a "spindleful" of thread.

The spindle as it is mentioned in the passage under consideration, and in this peculiarly constructed language, symbolizes diligence and industry. "She layeth her hands to the spindle, and her hands hold the distaff" is equivalent to saying "She is never idle," or as the Syrians say, "Her spindle is never out of her hands."

As a general rule spinning in Syria is done by the older women. It is often used as an occasion for diligent spinners "to get together." I recall very clearly the palmy days of my grandmother as a spinner, and some of the delightful spinning sociables she enjoyed with her peers. It was a delight to me to watch those good women lay their hands to the spindle. It is always delightful to watch an expert at his work. They worked with the ease and inerrancy of instinct. They spun while walking, talking, eating (informally) or even disputing. The only thing about the useful industry which I hated heartily as a boy was that when I came close to the feminine spinners the flying hairs from their whirling spindles fell on me, and "made my flesh creep."

Again the virtuous woman "Considereth a field, and buyeth it: with the fruit of her hands she planteth a vineyard." Here the language of the Scriptural writer is figurative. It refers to a good wife's thrift. She saves the coins she earns and treasures them in the well-known *kees* (money bag) in a corner of the clothes chest, where heirlooms and other precious objects are stored. In time of need she surprises her husband by the substantial sum of money she places in his hands, which enables him to buy a field or plant a vineyard.

"She is not afraid of the snow for her household; for all her household are clothed in scarlet." The marginal note greatly improves the translation by saying "double garments" instead of "scarlet." The Arabic version says *hillel*—that is, full, or substantial, garments. The snow is always dreaded by the common people of Syria. With it come no sleighbells and no skating. It is a time of stress (*dhieq*). The snow "blocks the roads and cuts a man off from his neighbor." At such a time, because of lack of fuel and adequate clothing, many of the people suffer. So the writer of Proverbs praises the "virtuous woman" very highly when he says, "She is not afraid of the snow for her household," because by her foresight and unremitting care she has amply provided for their comfort.

"Her husband is known in the gates, when he sitteth among the elders of the land." The Syrian husband of the good old type does not buy his wearing apparel "ready-made" at the clothier's. His garments are made by his wife. When he sits with the elders of the community in the market place or at the gate of the town where those dignitaries converse on matters of public interest, and speak parables and tell stories, his neat appearance bespeaks the diligence and loving care of his wife. "Verily his wife is a costly jewel," is the likely remark of such a fortunate man's admirers. How true also to the nobler instincts of the East are these words in this poetical description of the virtuous woman. "Her children arise up, and call her blessed; her husband also, and he praiseth her."

The closing words of this Oriental writer who lived long before the advent of "modern culture," reveal him as one of woman's truest friends and wisest counselors. "Favour is deceitful, and beauty is vain: but a woman that feareth the Lord, she shall be praised. Give her of the fruits of her hands; and let her own works praise her in the gates." This is the true "Order of Merit."

[1] Prov. xi: 22.   [2] Revised Version; ii: 10-14.

Part Six - Here And There in the Bible

During the time when the earlier chapters of this book were being published in the "Atlantic Monthly," requests came to the author from readers of those chapters for his comments on certain Scriptural passages which did not appear in them. Some of the passages suggested by those interested readers, I have considered in other parts of this publication. The other passages thus suggested, and others which presented themselves to the author during the progress of this work, but which for some reason or other he could not include in the preceding chapters, will now be considered, without the attempt to make of this portion of the book a coherent whole.

"And Abraham said unto his eldest servant of his house, that ruled over all that he had, Put, I pray thee, thy hand under my thigh: and I will make thee swear by the Lord, the God of heaven, and the God of the earth, that thou shalt not take a wife unto my son of the daughters of the Canaanites, among whom I dwell: but thou shalt go unto my country, and to my kindred, and take a wife unto my son Isaac." [1]

In the East the general custom is that the "speaking concerning a damsel" in behalf of a young man is entrusted to the most distinguished of his male relatives. Sometimes women are included in the mission. They approach the young woman's father and clansmen in a very dignified and formal manner, and, if possible, secure the "promise" for their son. It is only in rare instances that this significant undertaking is entrusted to one who is an alien to the groom's family (*ghareeb*) and who acts as an ambassador. Abraham was compelled to assign this duty to his trusted servant, because the patriarch had no relatives in Canaan. His demand from his servant to put his hand under his master's thigh and swear by the God of heaven and earth that he would do as he was asked is characteristically Oriental. The custom of calling upon God to "witness" a promise or a covenant between two individuals or clans is still extant in Syria. The placing of the hand under the thigh, however, is no longer done, but the habit of placing the hand under the girdle (*zinnar*) for the same purpose is generally practiced. However, it is the one who makes the request who puts his hand under the girdle of the one from whom the favor is asked. *Eedy tahit zinnarek* (my hand is under your girdle) means I come to you with the fullest confidence to do such and such a thing for me. In the eastern parts of Syria this practice is highly valued. Putting one's hand under another person's girdle is almost the equivalent of entering "under his roof" for protection from a pursuing enemy. If at all possible, the favor must be granted. I have no doubt that this custom is a survival in a different form of that of placing the hand under the thigh in making a solemn promise.

119

Abraham's experience upon the death of his wife with "the children of Heth" and with "Ephron son of Zohar," presents an interesting picture of Oriental courtesy. In the twenty-third chapter of Genesis, beginning with the third verse, the record reads, "And Abraham stood up from before his dead, and spake unto the sons of Heth, saying, I am a stranger and a sojourner with you: give me a possession of a burying-place with you, that I may bury my dead out of my sight." The burying-places in the East are clannish or church possessions. The Orientals, now as in ancient times, dread "a lonely grave." It is always expected that a worthy stranger be offered a burying-place for his dead in a sepulcher of the community where he happens to be, as that he should be offered the hospitality of a home. So we read, "And the children of Heth answered Abraham, saying unto him, Hear us, my lord: thou art a mighty prince among us: in the choice of our sepulchres bury thy dead; none of us shall withhold from thee his sepulchre."

That was noble of the children of Heth; they upheld the noblest Oriental tradition by their generous act. So also did Joseph of Arimathea when he took Jesus' body, "wrapped it in a clean linen cloth, and laid it in his own new tomb, which he had hewn out in the rock." [2]

Abraham, however, who expected to be a permanent dweller in Canaan, wished to have a burying-place of his own. So the aged patriarch said again to the Hittites (verse 8), "If it be your mind that I should bury my dead out of my sight, hear me, and entreat for me to Ephron the son of Zohar, that he may give me the cave of Machpelah, which he hath, which is in the end of his field." But Ephron would not be outdone in courtesy by his kinsman; at least he would not be accused of having omitted the nice formalities of such an occasion. "Nay, my lord," he said to Abraham (verse 11), "hear me: the field give I thee, and the cave that is therein, I give it thee; in the presence of the sons of my people give I it thee: bury thy dead."

To me this sounds "very natural." Ephron meant simply to be courteous. It is an Oriental custom to avoid a business transaction whenever a question of hospitality is involved, although it is not expected that the gift would be received as offered. The language on such occasions is purely complimentary. An Oriental offers to give you anything you may admire of his personal possessions, but as a rule you are not expected to accept the offer. Ephron did not really mean that he would give his field to Abraham without money and without price, but he would have Abraham know that he was ready to befriend him in his sorrow, and not to deal with him simply as a customer. The patriarch acknowledged the kindness by bowing himself down before the Hittites, but would not accept the field as a gift. Thereupon Ephron quoted the price of the field to the father of Israel in a truly characteristic Syrian fashion, by saying (verse 15), "My lord, hearken unto me: a piece of land worth four hundred shekels of silver, what is that betwixt me and thee? bury therefore thy dead." The gentle hint accomplished its purpose, "and Abraham weighed to Ephron the silver which he had named in the audience of the children of Heth, four hundred shekels of silver, current money with the merchant."

In speaking of the haste in which the Israelites were compelled to leave Egypt, the writer of the Book of Exodus says, [3] "And the people took their dough before it was leavened, their kneading-troughs being bound up in their clothes upon their shoulders." In the thirty-first verse it is said that Pharaoh "called for Moses and Aaron by night, and said, Rise up, and get you forth from among my people." As a rule the Syrian housewife kneads the dough in the evening in order that it may "leaven" during the night and be ready for baking early the next morning. The saying, "And the people took their dough before it was leavened," is meant to show that they departed before the early morning hours. Apparently the Israelites had wooden kneading-troughs such as at present the Arabs in the interior of Syria still use. The Syrians use earthen basins. What is called kneading-trough in the Bible resembles a large chopping-bowl, but is heavier and not so perfectly round as the chopping-bowl which is commonly used in the American home. In this basin the bread is also kept after it is baked. In the thirty-ninth verse it is said, "And they baked unleavened cakes of the dough which they brought forth out of Egypt, for it was not leavened; because they were thrust out of Egypt, and could not tarry, neither had they prepared for themselves any victual." The "cakes" are known to the East as *melleh*; this is the word the Arabic Bible uses. The *melleh* is a round cake or loaf about fifteen inches in diameter and about three inches thick. It is baked, unleavened, on the *redhef*; that is, hot pebbles. The fire is built over an especially prepared bed of small stones; when these are thoroughly heated, the *melleh* is placed upon them and covered with the live coals until it is baked. The shepherds in the mountains of Syria bake the *melleh* very often and think there is no bread like it in delicious flavor and sustaining quality.

It was such a "cake" which Elijah fed upon on his way to "Horeb the mount of God." In the nineteenth chapter of the First Book of Kings, the fourth verse, we are told that Elijah "sat down under a juniper tree: and he requested for himself that he might die; and said, It is enough; now, O Lord, take away my life; for I am not better than my fathers." It is of no small significance that the legend states that the Lord answered Elijah's prayer in terms of food. The prophet was both tired and hungry, so when he "lay and slept under a juniper tree, behold, then an angel touched him, and said unto him, Arise and eat. And he looked, and, behold, there was a cake baken on the coals, and a cruse of water at his head." We have no record that Elijah after he had eaten of the *redhef* cake, which was provided, no doubt, by the shepherds in that region for the *nasik* (hermit), ever longed for death.

In the sixth chapter of the Book of Judges, the eleventh verse, begins the story of Gideon, the "mighty man of valour," who delivered Israel out of the hands of the Midianites. "And there came an angel of the Lord, and sat under an oak which was in Ophrah, that pertained unto Joash the Abiezrite: and his

121

son Gideon threshed wheat by the wine-press, to hide it from the Midianites."

It is a prevailing belief in the East that spirits and angelic visitors appear especially under trees and by streams of water. Huge oaks are often found in burying-grounds and in front of houses of worship. "Rag trees" also may be seen in many localities in Syria. A rag tree (*shajeret-omm-shrateet*) is a supposedly sacred or "possessed" tree, generally an oak, on whose branches the people hang shreds of the garments of afflicted dear ones for the purpose of securing healing power for them. When the angel visited him, Gideon, we are told, was threshing wheat by the wine-press. The more correct rendering of the Revised Version and of the Arabic is, "Gideon was beating out wheat in the wine-press." As I have already stated, the grapes are squeezed by being trodden in a large stone-flagged enclosure, which is about the size of an ordinary room. As the harvest time comes early in the summer, long before the wine-making season, Gideon could use the clean floor of this enclosure to beat out wheat, with a fair chance of escaping being discovered by his oppressors, the Midianites. He was not "threshing." He was beating with a club the sheaves he had smuggled, before threshing time came when the Midianites exacted their heavy toll from oppressed Israel. Threshing is done with the threshing-board (*nourej*), which is called in the Bible the "threshing instrument." The *nourej* resembles a stone-drag. It consists of two heavy pine planks joined together, and is about three feet wide, and six feet long. On its under side are cut rows of square holes into which sharp stones are driven. It is these sharp stones which Isaiah, refers to when he says, "Behold, I will make thee a new sharp threshing instrument *having teeth*; thou shalt thresh the mountains, and beat them small, and shalt make the hills as chaff." [4] The sheaves are scattered on the threshing-floor about a foot deep; the thresher attaches the threshing-board to the yoke and sits on it, with his goad in his hand. As the oxen which "tread the corn" drag the heavy board round and round, the sharp stones cut the sheaves. In three days the "threshing" is ready to be sifted. The finely cut sheaves are thrown up into a heap and tossed up in the air with large wooden pitchforks. The breeze blows the chaff and straw away, leaving the heap of the golden grain in the center of the threshing-floor to gladden the eyes of the grateful tiller of the soil. To this "purging" of the threshing-floor—that is, the freeing of the wheat from the chaff and straw—Luke alludes in the third chapter, the seventeenth verse, where he says, referring to the Christ, "Whose fan is in his hand, and he will thoroughly purge his floor, and will gather the wheat into his garner; but the chaff he will burn with fire unquenchable." The reference to the burning of the chaff is meant to show its comparative worthlessness. I am not aware that the Syrian farmer always takes the trouble to burn the chaff, which is not easy to gather after the wind has carried it away from the threshing-floor and scattered it over acres of ground. The coarser part of it, which falls near the floor, is gathered and saved to be used in making the clay mortar with which the houses are plastered, and also sun-dried brick. We always went to the threshing-floor and secured a few bagfuls of chaff which we used in the annual plastering of the floor of our house.

Among the chief joys of my boyhood days were those hours when I was permitted to sit on the threshing-board and goad the oxen which carried me round and round over the glistening, fragrant sheaves. I often bribed the owner to grant me the precious privilege; and even now I should in all probability prefer threshing after this manner to an automobile ride.

In the seventh chapter of the Book of Judges we have a description of the simple process by which Gideon's army, with which he attacked the Midianites, was selected. The very honest record states that out of thirty-two thousand men whom Gideon had first mobilized only three hundred stood the final test. That test was very simple. In the fifth verse it is said, "So he brought down the people unto the water: and the Lord said unto Gideon, Every one that lappeth of the water with his tongue, as a dog lappeth, him shalt thou set by himself; likewise every one that boweth down upon his knees to drink. And the number of them that lapped, putting their hand to their mouth, were three hundred men: but all the rest of the people bowed down upon their knees to drink water." The three hundred constituted Gideon's army.

Bowing down upon the knees while drinking from a stream or a bubbling spring (*fowwar*) is the prevailing custom in Syria. This kind of drinking is called *ghebb*; that is, the sucking in of the water with the lips. But to strong and wary men this is disdainful. Such a prostration betokens lassitude; besides it is not always safe for one to be so recklessly off his guard while traveling, and to render himself an easy prey to lurking robbers. Therefore the men of strength and valor (*shijaan*) upon approaching the water assume a squatting position, lift the water with the hand to the mouth and lap it quickly with the tongue. This manner of drinking indicates strength, nimbleness, and alertness.

One of the most reprehensible Syrian habits is the mocking of those afflicted with diseases, or any sort of physical defects. I have no doubt that the afflicted of Palestine flocked to Jesus to be healed by him as much for the purpose of escaping the shame of the affliction as of securing bodily comfort. "There comes the one-eyed man ['*awar*]"; "there goes the limping man [*afkah*]"; "the half dumb [maybe one who stutters] is trying to discourse"; "the hunch-back is trying to class himself with real men"; "the diseased head [*akkra'*] is approaching, give way." These and other stigmatizations are very extensively current in the East. In the story of Elisha [5] it is said, "And he went up from thence unto Bethel: and as he was going up by the way, there came forth little children ["young lads," Revised Version] out of the city, and mocked him, and said unto him, Go up, thou bald head; go up, thou bald head. And he turned back, and looked on them, and cursed them in the name of the Lord. And there came forth two she bears out of the wood, and tare forty and two children of them."

What those children really said to Elisha was, "Go up thou *akkra'*." The *akkra'* is one who is afflicted with a disease of the scalp, a malady not uncommon among the poor people of Syria. Complete baldness of the head is spoken of also as *qara'*. It was this perhaps which the ill-mannered children noticed in the itinerant prophet. His cursing of the lads "in the name of the Lord" was no less an Eastern characteristic than their mocking of him.

As to the coming of the hungry bears out of the wood and devouring or tearing forty-two of those children, all I can say is that such narratives, which filled my childhood days, are deemed by Syrian parents to be the best means to teach the children not to be naughty.

In the opening verses of the fourth chapter of the Second Book of Kings we have the record of Elisha's kindness to a poor widow. "Now there cried a certain woman of the wives of the sons of the prophets unto Elisha, saying, Thy servant my husband is dead; and thou knowest that thy servant did fear the Lord: and the creditor is come to take unto him my two sons to be bondmen. And Elisha said unto her, What shall I do for thee? tell me, what hast thou in the house? And she said, Thine handmaid hath not anything in the house, save a pot of oil. Then he said, Go, borrow thee vessels abroad of all thy neighbors, even empty vessels; borrow not a few. And when thou art come in, thou shalt shut the door upon thee and upon thy sons, and shalt pour out into all those vessels, and thou shalt set aside that which is full. So she went from him, and shut the door upon her and upon her sons, who brought the vessels to her; and she poured out. And it came to pass, when the vessels were full, that she said unto her son, Bring me yet a vessel. And he said unto her, There is not a vessel more. And the oil stayed."

The belief in the miraculous increase of certain products, especially oil and wheat, is prevalent in Syria. In almost every community stories of such occurrences are told. Godly men and women, largely of the past, are said to have seen such wonders, and to have spoken of them to many before their death. Such blessings are supposed to come especially on the blessed night of Epiphany. [6] In the locality where I was brought up, the miracle of "increase" was said to happen in this wise: In some holy hour the cover of the jar of oil is thrown off by some unseen power and the oil begins to flow out of the mouth of the jar. The person who is fortunate enough to see such a sight must show neither fear nor surprise, but in the spirit of deepest prayer he must bring empty vessels and receive into them the increase. If he should fear or manifest surprise, the blessed flow would immediately cease, but if he receives the blessing in a spirit of gratitude and prayer the flow continues until all the vessels that can be brought are filled. But only godly men and women can see such a sight. Among the noble traditions of our clan is the story of one godly man of the Rihbany stock who witnessed the "miracle of increase" in his own storehouse. The flow of the blessing stopped, however, when his wife, who went into the storehouse to see why he was there so long, came in and threw up her hands in surprise at the strange occurrence. From childhood I heard this enchanting story, but I never felt deeply curious to investigate it until after I had gone to the American mission school in my native land. Then I sought the son of the "godly man" and begged him to tell me all that he knew about it. He assured me of his firm conviction that the miracle did happen in their storehouse when he was too young to see such wonders, and that his father and mother both saw it and spoke of it on occasions. At the time I became interested in the study of the origins of such narratives, both those good parents were dead.

But why allow shallow curiosity to weaken one's faith in the great spiritual principle which underlies all such beliefs? Attach all such pious tales to the Oriental's foundation belief that all good comes from God, and they become intelligible and acceptable. His intellectual explanations are faint attempts to grasp the great mystery of divine providence, to explain the ways of the Great Giver. If you do not attempt to make an infallible creed of these spiritual imaginings, they will serve as well as any intellectual devices to urge upon the mind the truth that ultimately "every good and every perfect gift cometh from above." Whether the resources were a few loaves and fishes, or thousands of loaves and fishes, it was God who fed the "five thousand," and it is he who feeds all the millions of his children through the annual miracle of increase in all the fields and vineyards of the world.

In his heart-stirring prayer, which begins with, "Out of the depths have I cried unto thee, O Lord," the writer of the one hundred and thirtieth Psalm says, "My soul waiteth for the Lord more than they that watch for the morning: I say more than they that watch for the morning." The Revised Version's rendering, "More than watchmen wait for the morning," limits the sense of the text, and, consequently, fails to express fully the phase of Eastern thought to which the Psalmist alludes. I have no doubt that the ancient poet meant that his longing for the manifestation of God was as keen as the longing of *el-mûtesehhid* for the dawn. This term comes from *sûhad* (sleeplessness). Eastern poetry is full of references to the *sûhad*, either from fear or other intense feelings like sorrow or love. In a land of tribal feuds and where wild beasts abound, the night is full of terror. *El-mûtesehhid* "wrestles" with the night, keenly observes the stars which mark the night watches, and restlessly watches for the advent of the day to dispel his haunting fears. The Arabian poet exclaims, "Oh, the night's curtains which are like the waves of the sea are fallen upon me, to afflict me with every type of anxiety. It seems that the Pleiades [which marked the march of the night] have been arrested in their course by being tied with hemp ropes to an adamant!"

It is not the watchman only that is meant here. He might watch keenly for the morning in times of fear, but the reference is to all those who watch for the morning in times of *sûhad*—a state which Orientals readily understand. The Psalmist would have that confidence and cheer in the presence of the Lord which come to the restless watcher of the night with the dawning of the day; that inward calm and peace which only the presence of God in the soul can give.

"Thus saith the Lord God, Behold, I will lift up mine hand to the Gentiles, and set up my standard to the people: and they shall bring thy sons in their arms, and thy daughters shall be carried upon their shoulders." [7]

The reference in these lines is to the custom of carrying the children in the East. The habit of carrying the children on the shoulders is, I believe, unknown to the West, but is universal in the East. In early infancy the little ones are carried in the arms. (The Revised Version prefers the word "bosom.") As soon, however, as the child is old enough to sit up alone, it is carried on the shoulder. The mother lifts the child and places it astride her right shoulder, and instinctively the little one clings to her head, where there is no dainty hat to hinder. The custom is so familiar to the mothers that often one sees a mother spinning or knitting with the child astride her shoulder.

As is well known, the message in the lofty strains of the later Isaiah is the glad tidings of the restoration of scattered and oppressed Israel. It is a prophecy born of Israel's ever-lasting hope that God will not cast off his own forever. So the prophet assures Israel in the name of the Lord that he will lead the alien peoples, not only to let Israel return to its own home, but to carry the children of the "chosen people" in their arms and on their shoulders, as do the servants of aristocratic parents. The prophet's hope of the restoration of his own people appears in the succeeding verse clothed in language which Oriental aristocrats love to use. It is the phraseology of earthly glory and a narrow vision of national destiny, which the New Testament liberates and enlarges. Says Isaiah: "And kings shall be thy nursing fathers, and their queens thy nursing mothers: they shall bow down to thee with their faces toward the earth, and lick up the dust of thy feet." Our world still has many grave faults, but it has certainly progressed since the days of Isaiah.

In the third chapter of St. Matthew's Gospel, the eleventh verse, John the Baptist, in paying his tribute to the coming Messiah, says: "I indeed baptize you with water unto repentance: but he that cometh after me is mightier than I, whose shoes I am not worthy to bear: he shall baptize you with the Holy Ghost, and with fire." The same thought is expressed in the somewhat different presentation in the third chapter and sixteenth verse of Luke's Gospel, where it is said, "the latchet of whose shoes I am not worthy to unloose." I have already stated elsewhere that to the Syrians the feet are ceremonially unclean; therefore it is very improper for one to mention the feet or the shoes in conversation, without first making ample apology by saying to his hearer, *Ajell Allah shanak* (may God elevate your dignity); that is, above what is about to be mentioned. In the presence of an aristocrat, however, no apology is sufficient to atone for the mention of such an unclean object as the shoes. Therefore, when one says to another, in pleading for a favor, "I would carry your shoes, or bow at your feet," he sinks to the lowest depth of humility. So when some of those who came to him to be baptized thought that John the Baptist was the Promised One of Israel, he humbled himself in Oriental fashion by saying that he was not worthy to carry the shoes of the coming Deliverer, or even to touch the latchet with which those shoes were tied to the ankles. In this last expression, the sandals, rather than the shoes, are meant.

The three evangelists, Matthew, Mark, and Luke, speak of the woman who was healed from a long illness by touching the hem or border of Jesus' garment. Luke's version is found in the eighth chapter, and the forty-third verse, and is as follows: "And a woman, having an issue of blood twelve years, which had spent all her living upon physicians, neither could be healed of any, came behind him, and touched the border of his garment: and immediately her issue of blood stanched. And Jesus said, Who touched me? ... Somebody hath touched me: for I perceive that virtue is gone out of me. And when the woman saw that she was not hid, she came trembling, and falling down before him, she declared unto him before all the people for what cause she had touched him, and how she was healed immediately. And he said unto her, Daughter, be of good comfort: thy faith hath made thee whole; go in peace."

The belief that holy persons and holy things impart divine power to those who trustfully and reverently touch them is not exclusively an Oriental possession. The Orientals, however, have always believed this doctrine. The woman mentioned in the Gospel followed a custom which no doubt antedated her own time by many centuries. The practice is followed by Orientals of all shades of religious opinion. As a son and adherent of the Greek Orthodox Church in my youth, I always considered it a great privilege to touch the hem of the priest's garment as he passed through the congregation, elevating the Host. To me the act was a means of spiritual reinforcement. I never would pass the church building without pressing my lips to the door or to the cornerstone of the sanctuary. Virtue, as I believed, came out of those sacred objects into me. The interpretation of the details of such records as the passage which is before us can be easily pressed too far. Such Gospel pictures should be sought for the general impression they make upon the mind, and not subjected to minute critical analysis as the reports of a scientific expedition. Jesus' reported saying, "for I perceive that virtue is gone out of me," refers perhaps to the belief that holy persons impart virtue or spiritual power to those who come in touch with them. Whatever really happened in Palestine nineteen hundred years ago, this belief is well founded. Whomsoever and whatsoever we love and reverence becomes to us a source of power. Many indifferent and merely curious persons touched Jesus, but nothing happened; for the *garment* possesses no healing virtues. But when an afflicted woman came to him with dearest hope and deepest prayer, the mere touch of his person reinforced her strength and revived her spirits. The Master indicated plainly that the healing power was not in the garment when he said to the woman, "Daughter, be of good comfort: *thy faith* hath made thee whole; go in peace."

In the story of the crucifixion [8] we read: "And as they led him away, they laid hold upon one Simon, a Cyrenian, coming out of the country, and on him they laid the cross, that he might bear it after Jesus. And there followed him a great company of people, and of women, which also bewailed and lamented him. But Jesus, turning unto them, said, Daughters of Jerusalem, weep not for me, but weep for yourselves, and for your children.... For if they do these things in a green tree, what shall be done in the dry?"

The saying with which the passage ends is current in Oriental speech in various forms. Of one who is greedy and voracious it is said (when the thing he eats is not very tempting), "If his tooth works so effectively in the bitter, what would it do in the sweet?" And, reversing the Scriptural saying, "If the dry is so palatable to him, how much more must the green be!" Again, "If one is not good to those that are his kin, what must he be to strangers?"—and so forth.

Jesus' saying to the women who followed him, "Daughters of Jerusalem, weep not for me, but weep for yourselves, and your children," facilitates the understanding of the closing sentence of the passage. He admonishes them not to lament the state of one who, though condemned, is utterly innocent, but the state of those who are so hard of heart, so devoid of human sympathy as to condemn one so innocent. With amazement he exclaims, "For if they do these things in a green tree, what shall be done in the dry?" If they deal so cruelly with a good and innocent person, what must be their attitude toward a real culprit.

The mention in the Gospel of the crowing of the cock recalls to my mind a very familiar Oriental expression. The shrill sound of the wakeful fowl always served us in the night as a "striking clock." We always believed that the cock crew three times in the night, and thus marked the night watches. The first crowing is at about nine o'clock, the second at midnight, and the third about three in the morning. The common people of Syria house the chickens in a small enclosure which is built, generally, immediately under the floor of the house. It has one small opening on the outside, which is closed at night with a stone, and another opening on the inside, through which the housewife reaches for the eggs. So "the evening crow," "the midnight crow," and the "dawn crow" can be very conveniently heard by members of the household. And how often, while enjoying a sociable evening with our friends at one of those humble but joyous homes, we were startled by the crowing of the cock, and said, "Whew! it is *nissleil* [midnight]." The hospitable host would try to trick us into staying longer by assuring us that it was the evening and not the midnight crow.

Now some "enlightened" critics assert that "in fact the cock crows at any hour of the night." Well, the critics are welcome to their "enlightenment." For us Syrians of the unsophisticated type the cock crowed only three times, just as I have stated, and thus marked for us the four divisions of the night.

The New Testament makes definite reference to the "evening crow" and the "dawn crow." As a rule the cock crows three times (separated by short intervals) at the end of each watch of the night. We are told that after the Last Supper, the Master and his disciples "went out into the mount of Olives," where Jesus said to them, "All ye shall be offended because of me this night.... But Peter said unto him, Although all shall be offended, yet will not I. And Jesus saith unto him, Verily I say unto thee, That this day, even in this night, before the cock crow twice, thou shalt deny me thrice." [9] This refers to the "evening crow," for the entire scene falls in the early evening. And so it was that when Peter did deny his Master in most earnest terms, "he went out into the porch; and the cock crew." [10] Again, while Peter was still being questioned as to whether he was not one of Jesus' followers, "he began to curse and to swear, saying, I know not this man of whom ye speak. And the second time the cock crew." [11]

The other passage [12] refers to the "dawn crow." "Watch ye, therefore: for ye know not when the master of the house cometh, at even, or at midnight, or at the cock-crowing, or in the morning."

In speaking of the speedy and mysterious "coming of the Son of man," in the twenty-fourth chapter of Matthew, Jesus alludes to the grinding at the handmill—a very common Syrian custom. The portentous saying in the forty-first verse is: "Two women shall be grinding at the mill; the one shall be taken, and the other left."

The *jaroosh* (handmill, literally, "grinder") has always been considered a necessary household article in Syria. [13] Our family possessed one, which, however, was shared by the families of my two uncles. The *jaroosh* consists of two round stones—an upper and a nether—from eighteen to twenty inches in diameter, and about four inches in thickness. It is a portable article. The two stones are held together by a wooden pin which is securely fastened in the center of the nether stone, and passes through a funnel-shaped hole in the center of the upper stone. A wooden handle is inserted near the outer edge of the upper stone. As a rule a strong woman can grind a small quantity of wheat at this mill alone. But as coöperation tends to convert drudgery into pleasant work, the women grind in pairs. The mill is placed on a cloth— something like a bed-sheet—or on a sheepskin. The two women sit on the floor, exactly opposite, and of necessity close to each other, with the mill between them. They both grasp the wooden handle and turn the upper stone with the right hand, while they feed the mill through the funnel-shaped hole with the left hand. The circular shower of coarse flour falls from between the stones onto the cloth or skin below.

At present the handmill is rarely used in Syria for grinding wheat into flour, which is now ground by the regular old-fashioned, waterwheel flouring mills. The *jaroosh* is used in the Lebanon districts and in the interior of Syria for crushing wheat into *bûrghûl*. The wheat is first boiled and then thoroughly dried in the sun on the housetop. Just before it is poured into the mill the wheat is dampened with cold water, so that while it is being crushed it is also hulled. The *bûrghûl* is one of the main articles of food among the common people; it is especially used for making the famous dish, *kibbey*. The whole season's supply of a family is ground in one or two evenings. The occasion is usually a very gay one. The neighbors gather around the mill, the men help in the grinding, and the telling of stories and singing of songs make of what is ordinarily a hard task a joyous festival.

The foregoing makes evident the meaning of the passage as used by the evangelist. "The coming of the Son of man," that great consummation of all things in the advent of the Kingdom, which the faithful disciples of Christ hoped and prayed for, was to be so swift and so mysterious that only the fully awake and watchful could have a share, in it. No one could tell who would be included in the Family Kingdom. For even those, who in this world sat as close together as "two women grinding at the mill," were not certain of being taken together. "Watch, therefore: for ye know not what hour your Lord doth come." [14] It is vain to deny that this watchfulness, this expectation of the sudden and mysterious coming of the Kingdom, has been a mighty factor in the development of the Christian Church.

Among my correspondents who have been readers of my articles in the "Atlantic Monthly," are those who are interested to know the attitude of the Syrian Christians in general toward the creeds and dogmas of the Church as they are known and accepted in the West, and also whether I would not enlarge the scope of this publication so as to include in it a discussion of certain doctrines which claim to have firm Scriptural basis.

As may be very readily seen, these questions involve the study of a complexity of subjects which the original plan of this book was never intended to compass. Again the author feels that it would be inexcusable boldness on his part to enter a field of thought which noted scholars and historians have thoroughly explored, and to pretend to discuss issues which only such scholars have a right to discuss. However, in compliance with the requests of those interested readers I will contribute my mite to the vast literature of a very old subject.

As is well known to church historians, the Syrian Christians of the Semitic stock have had very little to do with the development of the "creeds of Christendom." Theological organization has been as foreign to the minds of the Eastern Christians as political organization. They have always been worshippers rather than theologians, believers rather than systematic thinkers. Their religious thinking has never been brought by them into logical unity, nor their mysticism into full metaphysical development.

The Oriental has been a lender in religion and a borrower in theology. The course of religion ran from the East to the West, the course of theology ran from the West to the East. Had it been left to itself, it is certain that the Christianity of Palestine never would have built up such a massive structure of doctrine as the Athanasian Creed. Wherever the great doctrinal statements of our religion may have originated,—whether in Rome, Constantinople, Antioch, or Alexandria,—their essential parts were Greek and Roman, and not Oriental.

The Christian Church had its simple origin with a group of Jewish followers of Jesus Christ in Palestine, but it had its marvelous expansion and organization among the "Gentiles." In Palestine the faith of the Church may be said to have been instinctive, but among the Gentiles and under Greek and Roman influences that faith became highly reflective. Faith in God the Father, and in his Son (by anointing) Jesus Christ, and love of the brethren, constituted the simple creed of the Palestinian Christians.

It is not within my power, nor do I deem it necessary here, to trace the steps by which this simple faith was transformed into a ponderous, learned, and authoritative creed, whose essentials were finally fixed in the early years of the fourth century. It is sufficient for the purpose of this sketch to state that when the great doctrines which were wrought by the Ecumenical Councils were thus fixed, sealed with an "anathema," and backed up by imperial and ecclesiastical power, the churches which refused to accept them had but a very slender chance to live. The intention of those beneficent ecclesiastics and politicians who controlled the actions of the Councils was to do away with the schismatic spirit in the Church and to have "one flock and one shepherd."

Thus it may be readily realized that it was not very long after the crucifixion when the subtle mentality of the Greek and the organizing genius of the Roman began to assume control of the thought and practice of the Syrian churches. Excommunication, exile, and martyrdom swept away in course of time all obstacles out of the way of the "authoritative creed"; simple faith in Christ was forced to be hospitable to intricate scholastic statements of doctrine, and "love of the brethren" gave way, as a bond of union, to ecclesiastical authority. When the ambitious ecclesiastics of Rome and Constantinople finally brought about the great schism which divided Christendom into two bodies, known as the Eastern and the Western, or the Greek and the Latin churches, the churches of Syria aligned themselves with either the one or the other. The creeds became to those churches party slogans and means of division and hatred, and thus Christ was "divided," and those who claimed to be his followers, in both the Orient and the Occident, took up the cry, "I am of Paul; and I of Apollos; and I of Cephas." So the doctrines of the Syrian churches of every name are essentially those of the two great Roman Catholic and Greek Orthodox communions.

In answer to the second question I will say that I have refrained from doctrinal discussion in the present work; first, because so many of the speculative doctrines of Christendom have very little to do with the New Testament; second, because the central purpose of this publication is simply and purely to give the Oriental background of certain Scriptural passages, whose correct understanding depends upon knowledge of their original environment. I have deemed it unnecessary even to follow in the footsteps of the "higher critics" and inquire into the "genuineness" and "non-genuineness" of some of those passages. For the purpose of this work every Scriptural passage which reflects a phase of Eastern thought and life is "genuine." The aim of the author is that this book shall be as free from labored arguments as the simple statements of the Gospel themselves.

There is perhaps no phase of human thought which the Christian churches have not used in the advancement of their divisive creeds and pet speculative doctrines. There is an untold number of doctrinal documents which are now lying in the libraries of the world as repositories of moth and dust. They are of the earth earthy. The idea of universal brotherhood and human solidarity which is agitating the minds of men of all races and countries at the present time, is leading the Christian bodies back to the simple faith of Jesus of Nazareth, and causing them to heap contempt upon their technical subtleties and forced uniformities of intellectual belief. At least Protestantism is beginning to be sympathetically aware of its own precious heritage, and to feel the urging of its own genius. Free and coöperative individualism is winning signal victories over the unnatural authority of creed in the Protestant bodies, and the bondage of the letter is giving way to the freedom of the spirit. The Gospel of Christ is triumphing over the theories *about* Christ, and spiritual self-fulfillment by becoming Christ-like is crowding out of existence all theories of magical salvation. The creed of the theologians consists of many "articles"; the creed of Christ only of two,— "Love the Lord thy God with all thy heart, and thy neighbor as thyself."

I prefer Christ's creed.

[1] Gen. xxiv: 2-4.
[2] Matt. xxvii: 59, 60.
[3] Exod. xii: 34.
[4] Is. xli: 15. Revised Version.
[5] 2 Kings 11: 23-24.
[6] See my autobiography, *A Far Journey*, page 94.
[7] Is. xlix: 22.
[8] Luke xxiii: 26-31.
[9] Mark xiv: 27-30.
[10] Mark xiv: 68.
[11] Mark xiv: 71, 72.
[12] Mark xiii: 35.
[13] See Deut. xxiv: 6.
[14] Matt. xxiv: 42.

CPSIA information can be obtained
at www.ICGtesting.com
Printed in the USA
BVHW081436030522
635996BV00031B/2068

9 781789 872491